If I could recommenc
leaders, *RelationShift* w
and gets to the heart of what the church is called to be. Get a
copy. Study it. And discuss it with your team.

— Sean McDowell, PhD, Professor of Apologetics
at Talbot School of Theology, author of *So the Next
Generation Will Know*

In *RelationShift*, Jim Putman points us to the far-too-often-ig-
nored priority of authentic and loving relationships as the environment in which life-changing discipleship happens. Better
yet, he lays out a realistic and practical plan for pastors, leaders, and their congregation to get there. Since disciple making
churches start with disciple making pastors, this is a book I
highly recommend.

— Larry Osborne, Pastor and author,
North Coast Church

Since 1999 I have had a front-row seat to how Jim Putman
and his team planted and grew Real Life Ministries and all the
church plants and satellite campuses. It is one of America's great
church growth stories! I have been a personal recipient of what
a relationship is all about through my long-term relationship
with Jim and his wife, Lori. Relationship building and disciple
making is how the church should be built today! This book is a
must read by all pastors who are dedicated to growing a church.

— Douglas J. Crozier, President and CEO,
The Solomon Foundation

My good friend Jim Putman has done it again. He has hit the "nail on the head." Effective discipleship is not just the transference of content. God intended his transformational truths to be encased in incarnational community. Jim not only makes this point but gives leaders a blueprint to make this a reality in your church.

— Randy Frazee, Pastor and author of *His Mighty Strength*

We cannot separate the methods of Christ from the message of Christ. For more than two decades, I have had the privilege of walking with my friend Jim Putman and seeing him live out the life of a disciple maker. Jim is the real deal. He attacks the problem of removing relationships from the process of disciple making and how the results are divorced from the relational methods Jesus models. With strong application and stories of real life, I found *RelationShift* helpful and inspiring.

— Brandon Guindon, Senior Pastor,
Real Life Ministries Texas

Jim Putman's insights in RelationShift offer a stark reminder of how easy it is to slide into a sterile, ineffective discipleship routine. Through his insightful five elements, he takes us beyond shallow connections to biblical qualities upon which genuine relationships develop. Jim calls out the importance of gracious accountability with genuine support, none of which occurs in isolation. Jim perfectly balances "abiding" with "connecting" in RelationShift.

— Ron Hunter Jr., PhD, CEO of D6 Family Ministry

RELATIONSHIFT

Five Shifts for Disciple Makers to Live and Lead from Relationship

JIM PUTMAN
FOREWORD BY BOBBY HARRINGTON

a renew.org resource

To my parents, Bill and Bobbi Putman, who first showed me what discipleship and real relationships look like.

CONTENTS

FOREWORD

I t is easy for church leaders today to state that they believe in relational disciple making. In the ten years since Jim and I wrote *DiscipleShift: Five Steps That Help Your Church to Make Disciples Who Make Disciples*, I have noted a big change in terms of the language and descriptions that many, many church leaders have adopted.

I am grateful to God to see such a big change.

But for far too many leaders, this change is happening more in words than in actions, more sentiment than practice. In truth, relationships are hard work. We see relational difficulty in marriages, in families, in communities, and in places of work. Most people do not handle relationships well, especially the conflicts that are part of meaningful relationships.

This lack of relationship IQ is one of the most significant weaknesses in contemporary churches.

Think about it for a few moments. How many of the teachings of Jesus apply to relationships? How many parts of the epistles were written to address conflicts and difficulties? Lots of them, right?

Now think about churches today. How many church leaders handle relationships well—especially when conflicts arise, as they commonly do? In most churches, relationship problems and relational conflicts are simply swept under the rug.

Now let me take it one step further.

If you're a church leader, ask yourself, how do *you* handle relationships? How do you handle conflicts? What is your personal track record?

What about when it comes to your personal weaknesses and sin struggles? Do you have trusted Christian brothers and sisters in your church, in your close relational circles, with whom you can share your weaknesses, sins, and burdens? How transparent are you with others?

Too many church leaders feel all alone.

If you are like most church leaders, you have never been discipled in how to handle relational difficulties. Nor were you discipled in how to successfully deal with conflicts.

All of this makes leading today very, very difficult.

Many basic values that have guided America are falling apart. This chaos and confusion is creating conflicts like never before. And the basic fabric of evangelical Christianity is unraveling. The people in our churches and in our leadership circles are regularly polarized.

We need help. We need God's wisdom to help us develop a relational focus in our churches. We need to see ourselves as a part of a Christlike fellowship—where we love others and we ourselves, as church leaders, experience the love of others for us.

Jim Putman describes the path that we need, and he gives us the explicit practical tools that many of us lack.

In this book, you will find five key teachings that I have never seen brought together in one resource. In this book, Jim will:

1. Show you why fellowship and relationships are essential for the hard times Christians will be facing
2. Call you to a lifestyle of real love—and show you how to pursue it in your life and with your church
3. Show church leaders they can both provide fellowship for others and experience true biblical fellowship themselves
4. Show you how people develop trust for each other and how to become a trustworthy person for the other leaders in your church
5. Bring the whole relational emphasis of the Bible together for you as Jim describes the relational systems and procedures that have effectively propelled the church he leads (as well as many others)

This is not a theoretical book.

It is a practical book with proven biblical strategies and frameworks. Get your leadership team to read this book and work through the exercises at the end of each *RelationShift* section to help you and your team make the changes he describes.

This book has my highest recommendation. What Jim describes works. It has a proven track record. It will transform your leadership and transform your church.

— Bobby Harrington, CEO of Renew.org
and Discipleship.org

INTRODUCTION

Not long ago, I met with a major leader of a large Christian movement in a different country. This man and his family are the real deal. They love Jesus and are willing to risk for the cause of Christ in ways most of us cannot understand. God was reaching thousands through their ministry, and the numbers were mind-boggling. As we discussed their mission to make disciples rather than simply make converts, I was excited about what I was hearing. This ministry had gone to great lengths to teach truth to those they had won to Jesus. They had focused on evangelism and doctrine through their Bible colleges and were sending out teams to plant churches all over their nation. This team was excited about their progress.

As the conversation progressed, they asked me about what God had been doing with me recently in America. They had read some of the books I helped author (*Church is a Team Sport*, *Real Life Discipleship*, and *DiscipleShift*) and were wondering what I was writing now. I shared that I was working on a book about relationships for leaders because I was seeing so many pastors and ministry leaders who were exhausted and lonely. I had concluded that most Christians I deal with around our country are lonely as well. It isn't always obvious. It's a kind of disguised loneliness. They are very busy with a lot of people, but they have few relationships that are vulnerable and honest.

As I continued sharing, the group began to ask me questions about what my relationships outside of my family looked like. They asked me about my staff and elders, what we talked about and the kinds of things I shared with them. I was able to tell them how I was blessed to have several deep relationships within my church environment and that I would never have survived in ministry without them. At this point, one of the leaders (they were all from the same family) shared that she didn't have those kinds of outside relationships. In fact, she related more to the lonely pastors I was talking about. She went on to say that without the relationships she had with family in that room, she would never have made it. She said that there was not one person outside of that room she truly trusted, to which the rest of the family nodded in agreement.

Mind you, this ministry had thousands of staff members, volunteers, and pastors involved. As we continued to talk, the initial excitement they had expressed about what was happening through their ministry began to be replaced by a tiredness in their eyes. This amazing family began to show me what was behind the curtain of the large dynamic ministry numbers they were achieving. The spiritual battle was taking a toll, and they had been hurt deeply by some of the people they were working with.

At this point, I offered up a quick prayer to the Lord and hoped that the many hours of relational investment I had spent with them would give me the right to be able to say what I needed to say. I asked them a question in the form of a statement: "I thought you told me that you were making disciples here; it sounds like you are making converts." They looked at me a little confused, and I continued. I shared with them that, in my mind, discipleship is not just the act of sharing the gospel with unbelievers and then baptizing them. It's not just about teaching sound doctrine and equipping others to preach the gospel. And it's not just about teaching people how to start house churches in every town. It *is* about helping others learn to become great lovers of God and others. It involves learning to be faithful, loyal, and trustworthy. It means developing the characteristics of true spiritual friendship and love within the context of our spiritual family, the church.

The hard question then was, if those characteristics weren't present in the people they were discipling—to the point they couldn't trust them with their struggles and hurts—then were they truly making mature disciples? When we do our part to make disciples, it certainly doesn't guarantee everyone will become what they should be, but at least some should grow to become great spiritual friends with whom we can be honest and vulnerable—friends we can do life with. If we are truly making disciples like Jesus did, and we have the blueprint for maturity in the Scriptures and the Holy Spirit residing in us, our ministries should be producing the kind of people we can trust, love, *and* be loved by. Unfortunately, I had to leave my colleagues from the story above with the realization that even though their numbers were big, they weren't really making disciples in the way the Bible defines them. Instead they were leaving out one of the most important areas of all: the way they love each other.

Many who seek to make spiritual maturity the goal miss this essential relational core in their understanding of discipleship. Our God is a God of relationships, and Jesus said our ability to love each other well is a defining characteristic of a disciple (John 13:35). The mission to reach the world for

OUR GOD IS A GOD OF RELATIONSHIPS.

Jesus one person at a time is a mission of reconciliation between God and people—and then reconciliation of people with each other.

WHY SO LONELY?

So many church leaders are lonely. Why? Well, many pastors were taught in Bible college and seminary not to get too close to those they lead. They are told that if they do, they will lose their ability to lead because familiarity breeds contempt. Many believe that, since they must be "beyond reproach," they will lose their credibility if people see who they really are—people who have flaws. In fact, Barna Research reveals that 75 percent of pastors who struggle with depression never seek counseling.[1] Others say that if you really build relationships, it will hinder you from being unbiased so that you can make right decisions if conflict or sin arises. People may see you as showing favoritism to some over others in how you preach the Word and what you address.

These sorts of issues can arise, but the answer to them is integrity, fueled by the Holy Spirit and guided by God's Word. The answer to the problem isn't loneliness.

Many church leaders have worked so hard at conversion that they have not parented believers to maturity. This leaves most of their churches immature, and immature people hurt people. Thus, pastors and their families have been hurt a lot. So to insulate themselves, many keep everyone at arm's length. The problem with this is that as the head goes, the body follows. And when everyone in the church keeps each other at arm's length, people are easily shaken, remaining weak in their faith and having little accountability or support.

Relational volatility is especially prevalent right now in our crazy world. Isolation is one of the devil's primary goals because isolation from God and others can destroy us spiritually and emotionally, as well as make us suspicious of each other. Meanwhile, political polarization is finding its way into the church and bitterly dividing Christian brothers and sisters from each other. Busyness is keeping us from relationships so that even our free moments are filled with meaningless activity instead of relational investment. Many are trying to escape the emptiness through some sort of addiction. So many mental health issues are exacerbated by isolation.

Pastors, I know you see it.

You've felt it. And it's wearing down a lot of you.

So, sadly, it's not surprising when studies come out suggesting that 70 percent of pastors are looking for a new career.[2] There are multiple factors, but a big one is that the version of Christianity they are practicing is not leading to a connected, abundant life. If this is true for pastors, then what are the ramifications for those who attend the churches we lead? What about those who serve in leadership with these pastors, paid or unpaid? More than ever, we need to come out of isolation and become the relational people God wants us to be.

FROM *DISCIPLESHIFT* TO *RELATIONSHIFT*

Our small group in Northern Idaho began Real Life Ministries (the church) twenty-four years ago with the commitment to discipleship in relationship. When we began, we didn't have all the things people said we needed for a successful church launch. We had about three months' salary for two pastors, a converted garage to gather in, one guitar player, equipment for children's ministry that we bought at a garage sale, and little more. But we had relationships. Because I had never been in a big church, and because often we didn't have a building, we became accustomed to doing things in relational small groups. In those groups, we were committed to discipleship and raising up people to do more than they thought they could do.

From the beginning, we were committed to doing life together as Jesus' disciples, doing discipleship his way. Not only did we think his way was best, but it was all we had. From there, God led us to results I could hardly believe and would never have hoped to anticipate. Now there have been more than ten church plants, numerous missionaries sent out around the world, and thousands of disciples made.

Along the way, my team and I wrote books like *Church Is a Team Sport* and *Real Life Discipleship*. We developed manuals for training group leaders and books about chasing down prodigals. As a team, we helped start a couple of networks and provided lots of trainings for thousands of pastors. There has been a persistent hunger among church leaders for Jesus' model of relational discipleship that we were grateful to rediscover. Church leaders often ask us, "How can we do this at our church?" Push pause on that thought.

From those initial connections, a friendship with Bobby Harrington of Renew.org and Discipleship.org began, and together we wrote the book *DiscipleShift: Five Steps That Help Your Church to Make Disciples Who Make Disciples.* In it Bobby and I affirm that we believe Jesus' purpose for his church was to make disciples who would, in turn, make disciples. We also believe Jesus was the greatest disciple maker who ever lived, and his method is worth repeating. Not only is it *worth* repeating but also Jesus actually *expects* us to repeat it. *DiscipleShift* describes five shifts that teach how a church can make specific shifts to becoming a disciple making church.

So why *this* book?

Consider it a prequel to *DiscipleShift* that I didn't know we needed until recently.

Church leaders can launch wide-scale changes (think, "How can we do this at our church?") yet personally miss the *point* of them. They can even try to implement strategies centered on discipling relationships—yet bypass actual relationships in the process. When it comes to disciple making as the core mission of the church, I'm more committed than ever. But if you want to make disciples, you've *got to* make friends in the process. You've got to prioritize actual relationships. Otherwise, we're sunk. Without relational investment, disciple making is nothing more than just another program.

> IF YOU WANT TO MAKE DISCIPLES, YOU'VE *GOT TO* MAKE FRIENDS IN THE PROCESS.

This book walks you through five crucial shifts you and your church can make to ensure your church goes beyond just talking about relationships and becomes a family built on them.

In *DiscipleShift* we described the five shifts that church leaders need to make to empower their church to develop a disciple making focus. Now, in this book, *I describe the five shifts church leaders need to make to live out the relational focus needed for effective disciple making and to lead their church to do the same.* While the first book emphasized the organizational aspect, this book focuses on the relational preconditions that make disciple making truly happen.

I want to help you make these crucial shifts so that your church will focus on relationships the way they are modeled in the Bible. I will show you how relationships provide the environment for disciple making and how disciple making results in the fruit that God desires: people who love and are loved by one another. It sounds simple, but we can still miss this truth: we learn to be relational people *in relationships*.

REVISITING WHAT MATTERS MOST

In the DiscipleShift trainings we have regularly done, we ask leaders to put aside the mindset of a church leader for a few days. Instead, we ask them to think about whether they are actually making disciples themselves or just teaching and preaching in large groups. The truth is most pastors have never been discipled the way Jesus and the early church did it. In the conference, we go on to model an actual small group experience with disciple making as its focus. The small group itself is not the key; relational disciple making in small groups is what we're aiming to model.

These trainings have led to many life- and ministry-altering experiences. But as I would spend time asking leaders what they got out of the conference, all too often I heard things that weren't the point. We didn't hear the takeaways that mattered most. It seemed that we were not getting across the point we were trying to make about the necessity of relational environments. People did learn how to lead intentional small groups for the purpose of disciple making, but at the end of the day, pastors were still left lonely. In my view, this is unacceptable.

That is what led me to write this book.

My journey has been like a road trip. You follow the signs and keep moving on, but as you get farther down the road, you discover new signs that you could barely see from a distance. As you get closer, the signs become clear, and you make new adjustments. It does not surprise me that being involved in the *DiscipleShift* book and trainings has allowed me to see not only new insights but also old truths in slightly different ways. I am convinced that what we have taught is true, but with more experience and insight comes a deeper perspective. This book is my way of sharing the things I've learned now that I am further down the road as both a disciple and a pastor. I am excited you are reading it, and I hope that by sharing my thoughts, experiences, and examples, you will be able to see all that God has available for every believer when we make a few shifts in our thinking and our lives.

As we enter these five shifts, let me lay out the book's thesis: Overwhelmed leaders can't give churches what they need to mature. Immature churches can't give leaders what they need to survive. And neither one can nourish the other. For all our sakes, we must return to what Jesus modeled and the book of Acts described: genuine, love-giving *fellowship*. In the context of this fellowship, disciple making will happen. To get there, leaders must learn to live and lead from relationship. Discipleship deeply rooted in the relational way that Jesus modeled blesses our disciples—but it also blesses the disciple makers too.

SHIFT

1

From Feed Me to Fellowship

SOMETHING THAT FEELS SPIRITUAL—BUT IS KILLING US

The first of the five shifts that enable you to develop a relational focus and then lead your church in it is an emphasis on fellowship. Specifically, I am going to ask you to examine what it means for a church to think of itself in terms of being *a fellowship*.

First, a story. You've probably heard this story before, and because of this, you know how you're supposed to feel about it. If you're in church ministry, you may have even taught this story, and its implications might seem like second nature to you. Even still, I'm going to ask you to read the story again and assume that *you're* the one who needs to hear it.

AN UNIMPRESSED OUTSIDER

After leading his people out of Egypt, Moses led the Israelites to camp near Mount Sinai, where they would soon be given God's laws. While there, Moses' father-in-law, a priest of Midian named Jethro, visited them. When Jethro heard about all that God had done for the Israelites, he was pleased for them and impressed with Israel's God. The next day, Jethro was able to observe a typical day for Moses, as Moses took his seat as judge for his people. They would file through, tell him their issue, and he would speak to them about what they ought to do based on God's instructions.

This time, Jethro was not impressed. "What is this you are doing for the people?" he asked. "Why do you alone sit as judge, while all these people stand around you from morning till evening?" (Exodus 18:14b).

Moses' answer sounded spiritual: "Because the people come to me to seek God's will. Whenever they have a dispute, it is brought to me, and I decide between the parties and inform them of God's decrees and instructions" (Exodus 18:15b–16). The people were needy and knew whom to come to. They were hungry for direction and knew who would feed them.

We might have expected Jethro to respond to this explanation with something like, "Oh! That makes sense. Great to hear. Keep up the good work for God!" Instead Jethro was blunt: "What you are doing is not good."

Come again? Here's Jethro's explanation:

> What you are doing is not good. You and these people who come to you will only wear yourselves out. The work is too heavy for you; you cannot handle it alone. Listen now to me and I will give you some advice, and may God be with you. You must be the people's representative before God and bring their disputes to him. Teach them his decrees and instructions, and show them the way they are to live and how they are to behave. But select capable men from all the people—men who fear God, trustworthy men who hate dishonest gain—and appoint

them as officials over thousands, hundreds, fifties and tens. Have them serve as judges for the people at all times, but have them bring every difficult case to you; the simple cases they can decide themselves. That will make your load lighter, because they will share it with you. If you do this and God so commands, you will be able to stand the strain, and all these people will go home satisfied. (Exodus 18:17b–23)

You might be reading this and thinking, *Okay, first of all. I already know this story. It's about leadership delegation, and I already buy into the need for church leaders to delegate. Aren't we supposed to be talking about fellowship or something like that? Aren't there other stories in the Bible that are more about fellowship?*

Well, hang on. We'll get there. But first there's something we need to pick up from this story and carry with us the rest of the book. It's one of those insights you see only when you zoom out and look at the big picture. So let's zoom out for a moment. Jethro is not an Israelite. He may be related by marriage to Moses, but, being a priest of Midian, he's clearly an outsider looking in.

As an outsider, Jethro sees what the others can't.

What do I mean? For the Israelites, it makes sense, spiritually, for them to go to Moses with their problems. He's the guy who talks to God regularly. He's the guy who saw the burning bush, through whom God sent the plagues, etc. So spiritually speaking, who's the most appropriate guy to go to with moral dilemmas and questions about God's will? Moses, of course. That's what feels right spiritually.

Meanwhile, an outsider sees the obvious: this isn't sustainable. Moses doesn't have the time or energy to keep up with the impossible list of issues people will keep bringing to him day after day. It won't work. He won't be able to stand the strain. There are not enough hours in the day. What about having a healthy life for himself? Impossible. With that many issues coming to Moses day after day, that means no ability for him to deal with his own issues or the issues in his own family. That means no ability to rest and recover with those he loves. Messiness happens in every family, and Moses was going to wear himself out dealing with everyone else's messiness, unable to deal with his own. This was a recipe for Moses's family to grow resentful and distant from the mission to which God had called Moses.

The solution: Moses must bring people he trusts alongside him to shoulder these issues. Otherwise, saint or not, he's going to break.

Okay. Why start the chapter with this story? Here's why: If you're a church leader, you might have bought into a view of yourself that *feels* spiritual—and it's a view that makes sense to a lot of people within your church—but any outsider could tell you it isn't going to work for the long haul. It may feel right to see yourself as *the* pastor or *the* youth minister or *the* something else, and, as such, this is your mantle to bear alone. Sounds spiritual, right?

Meanwhile, anyone on the outside looking in can see how that movie ends. Lonely. Discouraged. Burned out. That path leads to awkward relationships with the people you should be closest with—the ones you didn't make time for who were supposed to be a support for you as well. You're absorbing pressures as if you were Frodo designated to bear the ring to Mordor.

And even if you as a leader aren't seeing yourself as the Moses in your church, a huge number of the people you lead are. And it feels spiritual.

It's not.

SO WHAT MODEL *IS* SPIRITUAL?

We were not equipped to be the whole team. Whether in life or leadership, we were made for deep relationships. The enemy we battle is so deceptive, working overtime in our culture. He's targeting us as leaders to isolate and convince us that we're better on our own. The apostle Paul describes "spiritual forces" in "heavenly realms" (e.g., Ephesians 6:11–12). When our eyes are opened to hints of the spiritual world around us, it becomes clear that we are not living in peacetime. Spiritually speaking, there is a battle between God and Satan over every person we'll ever meet—and that includes over us too. Every person is tainted by sin, and this creates a mess. The spiritual messiness we face means that we can't stay relationally unengaged personally and simply assume that our teachings and programs will do the trick for us, our family, or the families in the church we lead.

In the early church, we see leaders' lives centered on relationships. They stayed relationally engaged so they would not end up burned out and lonely. Exhausted people don't produce much fruit and don't look attractive to others. Why would we want what they have? So the early church leaders did life and ministry in relationship. For example, notice this snapshot of the way Paul did ministry: "Epaphras, my fellow prisoner in Christ Jesus, sends you greetings. And so do Mark, Aristarchus, Demas and Luke, my fellow workers" (Philemon 23–24).

Notice the way Peter did it:

> With the help of Silas, whom I regard as a faithful
> brother, I have written to you briefly, encouraging you
> and testifying that this is the true grace of God. Stand
> fast in it. She who is in Babylon, chosen together with
> you, sends you her greetings, and so does my son Mark.
> (1 Peter 5:12–13)

And the way John the apostle did too: "The elder, to my dear
friend Gaius, whom I love in the truth" (3 John 1). Of course,
they learned their method from Jesus himself:

> One of those days Jesus went out to a mountainside to
> pray, and spent the night praying to God. When morning
> came, he called his disciples to him and chose twelve of
> them, whom he also designated apostles: Simon (whom
> he named Peter), his brother Andrew, James, John, Philip,
> Bartholomew, Matthew, Thomas, James son of Alphaeus,
> Simon who was called the Zealot, Judas son of James, and
> Judas Iscariot, who became a traitor. (Luke 6:12–16)

As leaders, we do well not to see ourselves as the Moses
of our church. If we do, then what we need isn't for things to
slow down (as if they ever do). What we need is a clear-eyed
Jethro to remind us of the unsustainable path we're on. There's
a real spiritual battle going on for the people we lead, and they
need more from us than truth and direction from a distance.
From us, they need *us*. As Paul put it, "Because we loved you so
much, we were delighted to share with you not only the gospel
of God but our lives as well" (1 Thessalonians 2:8b).

But isn't sharing the gospel *and* our lives just another recipe for burnout? If we see ourselves as the Moses of the people we lead, then sure. But this isn't just for the people we lead. We need authentic relationships just as badly as anyone.

Remember the spiritual battle we've been talking about? It's not just being fought over those we lead. We too are in the devil's crosshairs. Let's stop pretending to be Moses and get back to pursuing what will lead to sustainable, sane leadership.

TURBULENT TIMES AHEAD

God knew we would need a strong core of faith to make it through the difficulties of life and the turbulence of church leadership, and he also knew that we need a team—a spiritual family—to help us make it through. You need more than biblical insights, leadership principles, and winning strategies. You really do need a spiritual family, or you're going to burn out.

This is something that takes intentional work on our part.

If Christians are to survive a turbulent culture, then we will need a faith life that is just as God designed it to be in Scripture. I've written before about the folly of trying to navigate class five rapids with an $8 Walmart raft. True Christianity is like a group of rafters who assemble the right equipment and all work together to navigate dangerous waters. Western culture has quickly moved to an anti-Christian position on many important topics, and most of us have discovered that we were not ready for it.

Some like to conflate "American" with "Christian," and this is not an accurate move. However, it's historically honest to acknowledge there are many aspects of a general Judeo-Christian worldview that have helped frame the Western perspective.

The West is increasingly post- and even anti-Christian in its popular views on many crucial topics. This matters because when people forget God, out-of-control lifestyles follow, and pain follows soon after.

Based on these trends, I believe that Christian leaders could be facing significant difficulties. Biblically, we are promised difficult times for following Jesus. Jesus predicted a time when evil will run unchecked and people's love will grow cold (Matthew 24:12). Paul warns that false teachers and ungodly times are coming when people will be lovers of themselves, lovers of pleasure, rash, conceited, and the like (2 Timothy 3:1–4). Based on my reading of Scripture, I believe we are living in such times now. If Christians are to survive with their faith strong, they will need each other—not just theoretically, but in actual, intentional relationships.

I believe what we are seeing is not only a lack of knowledge about what is true from God's perspective but also a lack of fellowship and relational discipleship in the lives of many believers. So not only are we lacking truth but we're also missing the mechanism that God gave us for passing along truth accurately, as well as practically. By discipling people, we help them let go of trusting in their own strength and values to develop a trust and faith in Christ that will be far more effective to carry them through life. It takes time, effort, and an intentional process led by a more experienced guide.

God's intention is that Christian fellowship will hold us together as we make disciples in the times we are now facing.

THE LEADERS THE CHURCH NEEDS

If you're leading others through this intentional process but don't have what you need to survive, this has a direct impact on everyone you are leading. If you are a church leader, you've got to discern what your people need and train them with the right information and skills *before* they come against the anti-Christian trends in this culture. Yet that only works if you live a spiritually healthy life yourself. Your job isn't just to *tell* those you spiritually care for that they need something better or to be prepared for challenges to come. Your job is to *model* what the right beliefs and actions look like. It's to *show* them what it looks like to follow Jesus in confusing times so they can learn and repeat the process with their own disciples.

> YOUR JOB IS TO MODEL WHAT THE RIGHT BELIEFS AND ACTIONS LOOK LIKE.

Leaders are equippers of the saints (Ephesians 4:11–14). If we show our people the perseverance and joy that can come with holding fast to the faith when the world is unraveling, then they will know they can survive and thrive as well. Together with the saints we have trained, we are able to rescue others who are struggling. Helping others navigate a confused culture becomes our best opportunity to reach a lost world in need of saving.

But drowning people cannot save drowning people.

As I mentioned earlier, many leaders and pastors today are lonely and discouraged. Often, they are disconnected from life-giving fellowship themselves. The survey of pastors I mentioned earlier suggests that it has gotten harder to be a Christian and harder still to be a Christian leader. With challenging issues of cultural vitriol toward Christian views, political divisiveness in the church, isolation, etc., many leaders wonder if it is worth it.

It is worth it. But to navigate what's ahead, we must return to some basics many leaders have left behind.

GETTING REAL ABOUT WHAT'S ON THE HORIZON

If we want to get serious about the turbulence ahead, we've got to face a very hard truth: In most cases, the people we serve were converted but not *discipled*. They want the church to "feed" them when they're feeling spiritually hungry—but not make them into actual disciples.

This is true either because we didn't disciple them, or they refused to be discipled. The resulting impact is that many believers are incredibly immature. This makes them vulnerable to even the moderate ups and downs of life, let alone a fast-moving, chaotic, and declining culture. As immature believers, they are easily angered and quick to point their verbal guns at anyone who is a leader—very often pastors in churches. These immature believers often won't listen to wise counsel, and they also won't do much proactively to live safer and more fruitful lives. They often see themselves as too busy to come to church. They are chasing after money or their kids or their hobbies, and they have no time for real and deep spiritual relationships. So they are isolated.

But they will certainly come out of isolation to look for help and support when their lives become what their lifestyle will inevitably reap. When life has thrown them around and they are left with wreckage, they begin to look outside themselves for help. They begin to realize they're spiritually hungry and look for someone to make them feel satisfied again—so they can resume life as usual. Most church leaders are trying to figure out how to help others, but many are overwhelmed by what feels like an impossible task, with many wanting to get out of the battle altogether. In their minds, they are barely holding on themselves; they can't take worrying about others too. It seems especially impossible when our people seem able to feed forever without growing.

WHAT WE'RE SUPPOSED TO BE MAKING

At our church, Real Life Ministries, we believe Jesus' mission led him to die on the cross for our sins. But that was far from his only mission. He cleared our sins out of the way on the cross so we could re-enter a reconciled relationship with God and then reconcile others with him as well. His mission isn't complete until we are making *disciples* who live out his teachings and tell his story, the gospel. What good is this true story if no one knows about it?

Jesus also sought to develop the kind of storytellers who would bring credibility to the story rather than detract from it. In my book *DiscipleShift*, Bobby Harrington and Scott Sagar's *Disciple Making*, and Brandon Guindon's *Disciple-Making Culture*, you will find a good articulation of the same vision, mission, and methods we use at Real Life, so I won't get into that here.

But I do want to take just a little time to share the definition of a disciple we use because we've got to be clear on what we're supposed to be making. The definition we use is found in the invitation Jesus extended to his disciples. In Matthew 4:19, he said, "Follow me and I will make you fishers of men" (ESV).

For us, this means that a disciple will *follow Jesus, be changed by Jesus*, and *join the mission of Jesus*.

1. We *follow Jesus*: we follow because we know who he is and because of what he has done for us.
2. We are *being changed by Jesus*: by the power of his Spirit and the Word of God, we are following his commands, which boil down to love for God and for others.
3. We *join the mission of Jesus*: we seek to not only *be* "fishers of men" but to *make* "fishers of men."

These three descriptors of a disciple give us clarity about the goal.

But there is something more that's crucial to note as we read through the Gospels. Jesus used a highly *relational* method to make disciples. He also more than implied that his disciples were to carry on his method. So later when Jesus said that his disciples were to now go and make disciples, he didn't mean for us to do it any way we want. The call was to go and do with others what Jesus had done with them. In keeping with Jesus' method, disciple making is a *relational* process.

DISCIPLE MAKING IS A *RELATIONAL* PROCESS.

If you've picked up this book and are already familiar with Real Life Ministries, then you're probably familiar with our church's relational discipleship method. You may have read earlier books or attended trainings. If so, thank you for letting us be part of your journey into becoming a more intentional disciple maker. But for many of you, I'm concerned you could be trying to implement principles while leaving behind the context that holds those principles together. I urge you to pursue the context where disciples are made, which is the topic of the next chapter: fellowship.

2

THE FELLOWSHIP

The first of J. R. R. Tolkien's *The Lord of the Rings* trilogy of books is called *The Fellowship of the Ring*. "Fellowship" means a plurality, and if you wonder if the book is well-named, just consider who the main character is. My guess is you'll have to pause and think about it. Yes, there's Frodo, the hobbit at the center of the quest to destroy the ring. But there's also the wizard Gandalf who leads the fellowship. Of course, Aragon, the future king, plays a leading role throughout the trilogy. And then there are times when the emphasis shifts to Frodo's loyal hobbit friend Sam, as the two act as more of a duo than a hero with his sidekick.

Shifting from a "feed me" mentality in the church to a "fellowship" reality means seeing ourselves as part of a fellowship. A church isn't meant to be a Tom Cruise *Mission Impossible* blockbuster; it's a *Fellowship of the Ring* epic in which even seemingly minor characters have a crucial part to play.

THE CHURCH'S DNA

Church wasn't the brainchild of a group of Christians who got together decades after Jesus' resurrection and ascension and wrestled with the best way to live out their faith. Church wasn't our idea. It was birthed from the disciple making methods of Jesus. Around Real Life, we explain that you can't divorce the person and teachings of Jesus from his methods and still get his results. Further, we teach that Jesus had a church in mind from the beginning. Church was imbedded within the DNA of his teaching and methods. Acts 2 (all of Acts, actually) is incredibly important because we see how the original disciple making commands of Jesus played out in the early church.

In Matthew 28:18–20 (as well as in Acts 1:8 and John 20:21), we see Jesus commanding his disciples to go into the world to make disciples by baptizing and teaching people to obey all of Jesus' commands. We then see in Acts 2 a great description of how the earliest church functioned. Let's look at the description in Acts 2:42–47. Notice how devoted to *relationships* they were:

> They devoted themselves to the apostles' teaching and to fellowship, to the breaking of bread and to prayer. Everyone was filled with awe at the many wonders and signs performed by the apostles. All the believers were together and had everything in common. They sold property and possessions to give to anyone who had need. Every day they continued to meet together in the temple courts. They broke bread in their homes and ate together with glad and sincere hearts, praising God and enjoying the favor of all the people. And the Lord added to their number daily those who were being saved.

There are Christians who want nothing more than to be fed by the church, and by that, they often mean inspiring events that make them feel spiritually satisfied. And yet this description of the early church shows us that something *far more* than an inspiring event is needed. It doesn't get more inspiring than the Pentecost event in the first half of Acts 2; the apostles were given the miraculous ability to preach the gospel to multiple nationalities with languages they didn't even know. The Holy Spirit brought the audience to a powerful conviction where they asked what they must do to be saved. No less than *three thousand* were baptized to form the church. What an inspiring event!

And yet we don't get to the fundamental point of church until Acts 2:42–27, where we see them *devoted* to the apostles' teaching, fellowship, the breaking of bread, and prayer. And did you catch the biggest focus of the passage? *Fellowship*. It's described with phrases such as "everything in common" and "continued to meet together" and "ate together with glad and sincere hearts."

This was not a picture of showing up each week to get fed, but of feeding *each other each day* with fellowship.

Merely attending an event was not enough, even a miraculous experience followed by teaching and baptisms! The apostles' teaching made clear that these newly repentant and baptized believers were called to obey Jesus' commands via the teaching of his trained disciples. Eventually the discipled would become the disciple makers and the church would grow as the messengers took his message to the whole world.

DEVOTED TO BEING A FELLOWSHIP

Let's take a closer look at Acts 2:42:

> They devoted themselves to the apostles' teaching and to fellowship, to the breaking of bread and to prayer.

The key elements of devotion for disciples, according to the Holy Spirit's design, are spelled out here in this verse. Notice that the people were first and foremost devoted to—committed to hearing and obeying—the apostles' teaching. It was because of their devotion to the apostles' teaching that they became devoted to the fellowship, the breaking of bread, and prayer. Their spiritual and social practices changed as a result of being devoted to the apostles' teaching. The apostles' teaching became the lifestyle of the believers. They were not just hearers but doers (James 1:22–25).

Let's focus on an aspect of their devotion that we often miss, even when claiming to base our churches on the apostles' teaching: the apostles' devotion to *the fellowship*.

The word "fellowship" is the Greek word *koinonia*. This word means more than getting together socially. It suggests having deep, intimate *commonality* (the root meaning of the word *koinonia*) in Jesus Christ. And it wasn't just a nicety added on to their faith when convenient. It was core to doing church. Their fellowship with each other was important enough that God wanted them to be *devoted* to it.

The early church lived out this fellowship in specific ways. They met in large groups (the temple courts) and small groups ("from house to house" in Acts 20:20). Acts reveals that they had close relationships as they traveled and worked together in the mission. Their fellowship included times of teaching and, as Acts 2:42 describes, their fellowship included breaking bread together (likely the Lord's Supper) and prayers. These elements were all crucial for the nurturing of these first disciples, and they all took place in the context of authentic fellowship.

They are still just as crucial for you and me.

THE FELLOWSHIP OF THE FAITHFUL

Let's take a deeper dive into their devotion to "the fellowship." In Acts 2:42, it's not just "fellowship" in the Greek text, but a devotion to "*the* fellowship." The fellowship of disciples with one another is essential for faithfulness, according to Jesus. The apostle John further describes fellowship in the book of 1 John.

> This is the message we have heard from him and declare to you: God is light; in him there is no darkness at all. If we claim to have fellowship with him and yet walk in the darkness, we lie and do not live out the truth. But if we walk in the light, as he is in the light, *we have fellowship with one another*, and the blood of Jesus, his Son, purifies us from all sin. (1 John 1:5–7)

Throughout Scripture we are told that the Word of God is like a light to our path. Jesus' teachings are the truth we need to navigate a chaotic culture. John explains that to walk in the light of God's truth leads to "fellowship with one another." It is that same word, *koinonia*, again. To be devoted to the teachings of Jesus is to become devoted to fellowship. You cannot have one without the other.

> **TO BE DEVOTED TO THE TEACHINGS OF JESUS IS TO BECOME DEVOTED TO FELLOWSHIP.**

The early church emphasized fellowship so much more than most churches do today. I believe we must shift from just feeding people each Sunday to an intentional focus on fellowship. We can't let our emphasis on teaching people what they need to know outweigh fellowship; this is precisely because true biblical teaching leads *to* fellowship. Devoting themselves to the teachings of Jesus is what formed the foundation for fellowship, as well as the ingredients that make fellowship possible.

THREE INGREDIENTS OF TRUE FELLOWSHIP

It's easy to read about how important fellowship is and think, *I get it. We need to hang out with each other more. I think I can manage that.* Yet even for the extroverts among us, what I'm describing—what we find in the New Testament—really does take an intentional shift. What kind of shift?

Let me emphasize the depth of the fellowship God wants us to experience in the church. The word that Scripture uses suggests deep and real relationships. (And speaking of "relationships," for the purpose of this book, I will often be using the words "fellowship" and "relationship" interchangeably throughout. "Fellowship" is more than an obligatory mingling of church people during events; it means deep relationships woven by shared experiences over time.)

As we continue reading this picture of the early church in Acts, we see three ingredients transformed their common interest in Jesus into true fellowship: time, focus, and honesty.

First, they *spent time together.* Real relationships require time, and they met together daily in some form or fashion. They shaped their schedules around the priority of Jesus and his people and mission.

Second, they shared a common foundation that was *the focus of their lives*: *King Jesus*. They were truly living as if Jesus was their king. They were displaying his reign through their acts of love. It's impressive the level of genuine care they showed toward each other. They met regularly, prayed together regularly, and even shared their possessions with each other when a crisis hit.

> There was not a needy person among them, for as many as were owners of lands or houses sold them and brought the proceeds of what was sold and laid it at the apostles' feet, and it was distributed to each as any had need. (Acts 4:34–35, ESV)

These actions naturally flowed from their fellowship with each other. The mission of God was propelled forward by people who cared deeply and compassionately for the good of many—rather than only for their own personal needs and wants. Later, we see the church organizing their leadership and resources to help the needy widows within the church. The church became better organized and strategic as they spent time together sharing their gifts, talents, and perspectives. Fellowship—real relationship—expresses care and leads to better work.

Third—many often miss this—you also see *authenticity and honesty* in their fellowship. Those with resources were only able to help when people admitted their need. Real fellowship includes the willingness not only to help others but also to *allow them to help you* during those times when it's necessary. This goes for the leaders too; we *all* need help from time to time. We *all* need fellowship.

In our book, *The Revolutionary Disciple*, Chad Harrington and I share our views on levels of maturity. Here they are in summary fashion:

- Lowest level: take care of me.
- Next up: I will take care of myself; you take care of yourself.
- Next up: I will help you, but I will take care of me.
- Highest: there are times when I can help you and times when you can help me.

Within the fellowship, there is honesty and transparency, rather than the pride that says *I* won't be the needy one.

IF *THEY* NEEDED FELLOWSHIP . . .

As we walk through the Gospels, we see Jesus in need. For example, he needed a place to stay because he had "no place to lay his head" (Matthew 8:20). We see people sharing their resources with him, such as the women who provided for his and his disciples' financial needs (Luke 8:1–3). The evening of his arrest, we see Jesus in the garden of Gethsemane asking his disciples to pray for him because his soul was "overwhelmed with sorrow to the point of death" (Matthew 26:38). We see Jesus sending his disciples into towns without even an extra set of clothes or money so that they would need to be cared for by those who would accept their message. Later, in Acts and Paul's letters, we see Paul receiving help from churches who provided for his personal needs. We see churches sharing when there was a need with other churches.

Fellowship requires mutual sharing of needs and gifts. True fellowship means that we tell each other the truth about what we're going through. We carry one another's burdens—which means we need to know what those burdens are. We confess our struggles and sins to one another. We come to know others and allow them to know us so that we can experience the life we were meant to have in Christ. We see this honesty-fueled fellowship all through the early church. Yet

FELLOWSHIP REQUIRES MUTUAL SHARING OF NEEDS AND GIFTS.

today, it seems that we are too busy, too proud, or too uncaring to have that kind of fellowship. Have we stopped needing it? No, and our lack of fellowship is emaciating us.

Our lack of fellowship is also obstructing our mission. Jesus sent the disciples out in pairs and so did the early church. They shared needs and abilities in relationships, and it was in these relationships that they carried out the mission to reach the world. People who are reconciled to God in Christ are reconciled to one another in relationship as we carry out the ministry of reconciliation to the world that desperately needs it.

Let's be the people described throughout the New Testament. Let's shift from being a burnt-out few trying to feed the rest to being a community of deep fellowship with each other that learns to both give and receive support.

A SNAPSHOT OF THE SHIFT

About three years ago, John (not his real name) was in my new coaching group in the Relational Discipleship Network. It was our first meeting via video conferencing, and we were all sharing a bit about our journey to this point. John shared that he and his wife had come to a DiscipleShift training at a time when they had been ready to quit the ministry. He shared that he had been "that pastor" I had talked about in the question-and-answer time in the two-day experience.

In that session, I shared that so many pastors are exhausted, lonely, and discouraged. They are so busy taking care of all the counseling sessions, weddings, funerals, preaching, and constant conflict resolution that they even have shallow relationships at home caused by exhaustion and lack of time. Wives go without their husbands, kids without their fathers, and these pastors go without healthy lifestyles or close relationships.

John told me his wife had cried during the talk and kept looking over at him because they had had this struggle for as long as he had been in ministry (twenty-five years), and she had about had it. In the video call, he shared that during the training, he had gotten a glimpse of a different way of doing ministry, and he wanted to discover it. Having a life filled with peace and real friends and a shared ministry approach looked so good. But he admitted that, if left to himself, he didn't even know where to start.

Fast forward.

This last year, our Relational Discipleship Network team was doing a conference where we shared what the Lord had taught us all. John and his wife, still in the network, came to say hi because we were in their area. John looked so different, and so did his wife. They were smiling, and he was back to being excited about his church and all that God was doing in his family and ministry. He shared about the new staff he had raised up and how they were working together. He shared how his eldership had changed and were sharing real life together. It was so encouraging.

So what had he changed in the last few years?

CONCRETE STEPS TOWARD FELLOWSHIP

There are some very important steps that must be taken by the leader if the church is to become the fellowship that God intended. Let me list some of those that John had to take. But remember, none of these are mere tasks to be checked off a list, but rather changes in your life that take time and intentionality.

Redefining maturity. The pastor had to start recasting what spiritual maturity meant for the congregation. His role was to be an equipper rather than the one playing all roles. This meant he had to start with his elders, then key volunteers, and then the church. He had to learn to say no so that he could actually put his life in order. He had to admit that doing the job the old way was stealing his life.

Carving new patterns. John needed to surround himself with the people who would keep him on track. There were default patterns that he had settled into without thinking. He didn't want to fall back into these, so he needed a counselor to help him figure out what was driving him to say yes to everyone. He had to work out the difference between saying no to God and saying no to the church. He also needed a network where he could be coached (including challenged) to stay the course. People can be so convincing and can maneuver you to meet their perceived needs for them rather than taking their own responsibility themselves.

Creating a group. The pastor had to decide to start a group where he was going to shift from primarily feeding others (i.e., a transfer of information) to mutual fellowship. It's more than just this (as we will explore in future chapters), but it can't be less. Disciple making is not just about creating a band of brothers that help you do life; it's also a reproductive process that teaches others to do the same with others. Without both, we either become a clique that doesn't care about others or an exhausting missional machine that wears us out. Again, the word *koinonia* is more than just a social gathering. John had to clarify that this group was going to be more focused than what "fellowship" often means to people. He had to make it clear what the new rules for this group would be. It would involve real honesty and accountability, with plenty of "I" statements, not just abstract generalities.

John had been terrified to tell his group that he was dealing with depression because to him, it implied weakness and an inability to lead because of his own brokenness. What he found was that, rather than being judged and left behind, these guys began to feel closer to him than ever before. He now had emotional support. Through this, they all learned that God could use even broken people, and this caused them all to think through their individual reasons for not serving with their gifts. The devil loves to tell us we are unworthy of true fellowship, which leads us to hide our failings or allow them to keep us from serving altogether. John learned that as he shared his "stuff," the other guys desired to help him carry the burden. They became teammates who started to share the hurts and the work together.

We desperately need the fellowship that characterized the early church. We need to be devoted to time, focus, and honesty with each other—not as a periodic add-on when it's convenient, but as the context in which our faith can survive and grow.

And it's in the context of fellowship that we learn and practice our next shift: genuine love, one for another.

A FELLOWSHIP EMPHASIS EXERCISE

How are you doing in the area of fellowship? The New Testament is full of descriptions of how we in the church are to be there for each other in real fellowship. Many of these descriptions are stated as "one another" passages (e.g., "love one another," "serve one another," etc.). The following is a list of thirty-nine "one another's" from the New Testament. For a full list of fifty-nine "one another" Scriptures (including duplicates), see Appendix A: Fifty-Nine "One Another's" in the New Testament.

Read the following list and then mark the ten "one another's" that you most often experience within your church context (e.g., with a check mark). Then mark the ten "one another's" that you least often experience (e.g., with an X). Share the lists with your leadership group and share your thoughts and feelings about the least often experienced list of "one another's."

_____ 1. "Be at peace with each other" (Mark 9:50b).
_____ 2. "Wash one another's feet" (John 13:14b).
_____ 3. ". . . Love one another . . ." (John 13:34).
_____ 4. "Be devoted to one another in love" (Romans 12:10a).
_____ 5. "Honor one another above yourselves" (Romans 12:10b).

_____ 6. "Live in harmony with one another"
(Romans 12:16a).

_____ 7. "Stop passing judgment on one another"
(Romans 14:13a).

_____ 8. "Accept one another, then, just as Christ accepted
you" (Romans 15:7a).

_____ 9. "Instruct one another" (Romans 15:14b).

_____ 10. "Greet one another with a holy kiss"
(Romans 16:16a).

_____ 11. "When you gather to eat, you should all eat together"
(1 Corinthians 11:33b).

_____ 12. "Have equal concern for each other"
(1 Corinthians 12:25b).

_____ 13. "Serve one another humbly in love"
(Galatians 5:13b).

_____ 14. "If you bite and devour each other . . . you will be
destroyed by each other" (Galatians 5:15).

_____ 15. "Let us not become conceited, provoking and
envying each other" (Galatians 5:26).

_____ 16. "Carry each other's burdens" (Galatians 6:2a).

_____ 17. "Be patient, bearing with one another in love"
(Ephesians 4:2b).

_____ 18. "Be kind and compassionate to one another"
(Ephesians 4:32a).

_____ 19. ". . . Forgiving each other . . ." (Ephesians 4:32)

_____ 20. "Speak to one another with psalms, hymns and songs
from the Spirit" (Ephesians 5:19a).

_____ 21. "Submit to one another out of reverence for Christ"
(Ephesians 5:21).

_____ 22. "In humility value others above yourselves" (Philippians 2:3b).

_____ 23. "Do not lie to each other" (Colossians 3:9a).

_____ 24. "Bear with each other" (Colossians 3:13a).

_____ 25. ". . . Forgive one another if any of you has a grievance against someone . . ." (Colossians 3:13).

_____ 26. "Let the message of Christ dwell among you richly as you teach . . . one another" (Colossians 3:16a).

_____ 27. "Admonish one another" (Colossians 3:16b).

_____ 28. "Make the Lord make your love increase and overflow for each other" (1 Thessalonians 3:12a).

_____ 29. "Build each other up" (1 Thessalonians 5:11b).

_____ 30. "Encourage one another daily" (Hebrews 3:13a).

_____ 31. "Spur one another on toward love and good deeds" (Hebrews 10:24b).

_____ 32. "Do not slander one another" (James 4:11a).

_____ 33. "Don't grumble against one another" (James 5:9a).

_____ 34. "Confess your sins to each other" (James 5:16a).

_____ 35. "Pray for each other . . ." (James 5:16b).

_____ 36. "Love one another deeply, from the heart" (1 Peter 1:22b).

_____ 37. "Offer hospitality to one another without grumbling" (1 Peter 4:9).

_____ 38. "Each of you should use whatever gift you have received to serve others" (1 Peter 4:10a).

_____ 39. "Clothe yourselves with humility toward one another" (1 Peter 5:5).

SHIFT 2

From Friendliness to Love

3

BEYOND FRIENDLINESS

Whether it's getting fast food, grabbing a coffee, or going to the bank, it's funny how even "drive-thru's" can feel long. They're supposed to be the fastest way yet invented to make these kinds of transactions. But because of people's general grumpiness about having to wait in lines, many of these companies have trained their employees to be as friendly and accommodating as possible. "How are you today? Oh, that's great . . . No problem, take your time . . ." Maybe these employees are genuinely nice. But they're not being friendly because they're trying to cultivate friendship with customers; a drive-thru line doesn't make room for that. They're trained to be friendly because satisfied customers keep coming back. Using a friendly script and friendly tone helps them keep their business.

There are some churches out there that bark at strangers and could use some basic training in friendliness, but most churches I'm connected with are friendly and warm toward visitors. That's good. But friendliness can be done in a hurry. It's something we've come to expect from basically every place we do business with. So when a church offers friendliness, what's to prevent the people who visit from seeing our friendliness as just another script to keep people coming back?

We need to move beyond just being friendly. We need to return to what makes us unique: *love*. As Jesus said, "By this everyone will know that you are my disciples, if you love one another" (John 13:35). For this to be our clearest distinguishing characteristic, it's obvious that love means something much deeper than giving people warm and friendly customer service.

WHAT WAS MISSING IN THE CORINTHIAN CHURCH?

As a commissioned apostle, Paul understood the big relational story of God and planet Earth. He saw that his role was to make disciples who would become mature in Christ. Paul wrote it this way in Colossians 1:28: "He is the one we proclaim, admonishing and teaching everyone with all wisdom, so that we may present everyone fully mature in Christ."

So when Paul saw immaturity in his disciples, he dealt with it quickly and persistently. Every one of his letters dealt with disciples forgetting who they were called to be or being downright rebellious in one way or another. The book of 1 Corinthians is a tough-minded letter written to a group that was fighting over almost everything.

The book starts off warm enough ("Grace and peace to you . . . . I always thank my God for you . . ."). But by a few verses in, he's gone way beyond mere friendliness. He's describing serious issues they've got in their church, saying, "C'mon, guys!"

- They were splintering into factions (1 Corinthians 1:10).
- They were jealous of each other (1 Corinthians 3:3).

- They were permissive when it came to sexual immorality (1 Corinthians 5:1–6).
- They were suing each other (1 Corinthians 6:1–6).
- Some were overeating while others went hungry in church meals (1 Corinthians 11:17–22).

Paul loved this church. And love goes way beyond customer service. Love is concerned with people's eternal outcome, not just whether they keep coming back to church.

This context helps make sense of the most beloved section of 1 Corinthians, the "love chapter" of 1 Corinthians 13. Let's take a look at the opening lines of the chapter. Paul has been describing spiritual behaviors the Corinthian church had accepted as the most important. Yet having spiritual gifts and impressive abilities and intellectual capacities can all be worthless if they're divorced from love:

> If I speak in the tongues of men or of angels, but do not have love, I am only a resounding gong or a clanging cymbal. If I have the gift of prophecy and can fathom all mysteries and all knowledge, and if I have a faith that can move mountains, but do not have love, I am nothing. If I give all I possess to the poor and give over my body to hardship that I may boast, but do not have love, I gain nothing. (1 Corinthians 13:1–3)

Why did Paul double down on the importance of love? Not only did he underscore its importance in the strongest language possible, he also went on to describe what love looks like so his readers wouldn't have something less in mind:

> Love is patient, love is kind. It does not envy, it does not
> boast, it is not proud. It does not dishonor others, it is not
> self-seeking, it is not easily angered, it keeps no record of
> wrongs. Love does not delight in evil but rejoices with
> the truth. It always protects, always trusts, always hopes,
> always perseveres. (1 Corinthians 13:4–7)

So why did Paul make love such a central focus for the
Corinthian church?

It's because love is what will solve their problems! Factions,
jealousy, permissiveness, lawsuits, drunkenness, ignoring people's hunger—what the church needed more than anything was
to learn to love. Miraculous gifts and intellectual abilities may
have felt like hallmarks of spirituality, but true spiritual maturity meant they were growing in love.

Your church might have compelling programing, impressive teaching, and friendly service. Without love, you've got
nothing. Spiritual maturity means refocusing on the core of
Christian maturity: Jesus-style love.

The idea of loving others as a core sign of spiritual maturity
is found throughout the Bible. Notice what it was that kept the
Corinthian Christians immature (hint: it wasn't lack of basic
Bible knowledge):

> Brothers and sisters, I could not address you as people
> who live by the Spirit but as people who are still
> worldly—mere infants in Christ. I gave you milk, not
> solid food, for you were not yet ready for it. Indeed,
> you are still not ready. You are still worldly. For since
> there is jealousy and quarreling among you, are you

> not worldly? Are you not acting like mere humans?
> (1 Corinthians 3:1–3)

RECOGNIZING REAL LOVE

You can recognize real love by its tenacity. Friendliness makes people happy for the moment, whereas love keeps after people for the long haul.

I know a man who got involved in an affair with another woman. He had been regularly involved in a church plant. But he felt like he could not give up on the affair because he was so infatuated with this woman. His wife

LOVE KEEPS AFTER PEOPLE FOR THE LONG HAUL.

resolved, after many attempts, that she could no longer stay married. It broke her heart, but she was planning on a divorce.

Because the leadership of the new church loved this man so much, they reached out to him. There were multiple conversations. For a period of months, he withdrew from the church, but the leadership of the church kept him in their hearts and prayers.

Finally, the lead pastor's wife ran into him in a grocery store and told him that she and her husband still loved him. It was a simple but genuine interaction. His heart started to soften. Then he met again with the pastor from the church plant. They had a long conversation. Finally, this man asked the pastor if he could meet with the woman he was involved with because he did not have the strength to break off the relationship himself.

Could the pastor help him break off the affair?

The pastor loved this man and his wife so much that he decided to meet with the woman. He described it as one of the strangest meetings that he had ever experienced. At first the woman was surprised. Then she got angry. Then she stormed out of the meeting.

But she never interacted with the man she was having an affair with again.

The wife eventually accepted him back. They went to counseling (the church helped pay for it).

It was love for the pastor to reach out to the man involved in the affair. It was love to keep meeting with him multiple times. It was love when the pastor's wife ran into this man at the grocery store and reminded him that he wasn't forgotten. It was love that compelled these leaders to tell this man the truth of his sin. And it was love that led the pastor to put himself in the uncomfortable position of personally talking to the woman involved in the affair.

And it was love that led his wife to accept him back.

The marriage was restored, and their children's lives were blessed. He rebuilt his reputation and trustworthiness after many years. Decades later, this man is now an elder at the same church. The grace he needed and received is the same kind of grace he regularly now shares with others.

Mere friendliness would have said, "I hope you're happy in your new relationship." Love said, "We miss you. What can we do to help you get right with God?"

DEFINITIONS MATTER

Progressive or liberal churches may also teach that discipleship leading to love is the most important goal. However, most of them have redefined love to mean that we not only love the sinner but we also *accept* the sin as well. It's easy to skip the part that tells us that if we love Jesus, we will obey his commands (John 14:15). In the effort to reach lost people and gain the world's approval, they determine it's best to just tell them about a loving Savior—and not about a righteous judge. To them love is more like indifferently affirming their choices regardless of how they turn out.

Of course, this isn't biblical discipleship at all.

In other cases, people define love according to a social gospel that focuses on righting the injustices of the world via social justice efforts. In this case, loving disadvantaged people and ministering to their physical needs are what being a disciple is all about. It's important to help meet people's physical needs. But just caring about the physical needs and not dealing with the spiritual, eternal realities only makes people more comfortable until they one day face judgment for their sins—without a Savior.

Real love goes beyond affectionate feelings. Or friendly words. Or best wishes.

Typically, even in the church, when people say they love something, they mean they feel fondness for a person, place, or thing that makes them happy. They get a strong feeling of longing or excitement. They love something because there's a perceived benefit to them. They love another person because that person is kind, funny, or treats them well and ultimately makes them feel good about themselves. This happens in marriages all the time when marriage is built on happy feelings. When the feelings fade, a spouse says something like, "I just don't love them anymore."

But is that all love is? What happens when you love somebody and they let you down? Or someone stops being all you hoped they would be? Or never lives up to your expectations? What then?

A CROSS-SHAPED *ACTION*

The word "love" gets used all the time, but most people have long lost what love actually means. Or, perhaps we could say, what love actually *does*. This is because love isn't just words. It isn't just feelings. It's action.

In our churches, we need to shift back to a clear, simple, biblical definition of love.

We know there are different words in the Greek New Testament for love. There is *philia* (brotherly love), *eros* (romantic love), and *storge* (family love). For this discussion, I am going to focus on *agape,* the word for love most often used in the New Testament for the way Christians treat others and treat themselves.

It's what Paul defines and describes in 1 Corinthians 13:4–7, where he explains that love is patient and kind, and that it doesn't envy, boast, get easily angered, or keep record of wrongs. These descriptions presuppose that love isn't easy. In fact, it's when we have opportunities to get impatient, envious, angered, etc., that we know it's an opportunity to show love. We grow in love when the other person isn't being lovable.

> **WE GROW IN LOVE WHEN THE OTHER PERSON ISN'T BEING LOVABLE.**

When we're thinking straight, it's clear to us that God doesn't just love us because we're lovable and we give him happy feelings: his love for us involves sacrificial action regardless of our unworthiness of it. Yet when it comes to our love for other people, we somehow assume that love is strongest when the other person is making us feel happy. I am so glad that our God continues to pour grace into my life even as I constantly struggle to be all he saved me to be. He did not give me a one-time deposit of grace but keeps pouring into my life.

In his book, *Kingdom Life* (a part of Renew.org's *Real Life Theology* series), Atlanta-area minister Kelvin Teamer defines love as "a cross-shaped action that glorifies God and benefits someone else."[3] This is a helpful definition because it brings in both the vertical and horizontal dimensions of real love. Based on God's love for us, we follow his example in doing actions for each other that glorify God and help them out. This honors Jesus' "greatest command," which says love for God is our top priority, followed by loving people as we love ourselves (Mark 12:29–31).

Think about that. Love doesn't come in a sentimental heart shape. It comes in the shape of a cross, as we do things for others that truly help them (horizontal) and glorify God (vertical). In the next chapter, we'll look at concrete ways you can shift to cross-shaped love as you live and lead from relationship.

4

LOVE IS A FIGHTING WORD

Romans 12:9 teaches a fascinating truth about love. Here's the verse: "Love must be sincere. Hate what is evil; cling to what is good." The first sentence here literally says that *agape* must be without "hypocrisy." The word "hypocrisy" is the cheap imitation of genuine action; it's merely an "act." A hypocrite was a stage actor. So Romans 12:9 tells us how our love for others can prove to be more than just an act. Here's how: "Hate what is evil; cling to what is good."

What Paul is saying is that if we *genuinely* love people (and we're not just *acting* as if we do), we will do two things:

1. Hate what is evil.
2. Cling to what is good.

But isn't hate a bad thing? It's not bad at all—if you're hating the thing that destroys the person you love. Doctors aren't bad doctors for seeking to destroy cancer; they seek to destroy cancer because they are trying to save the thing that the cancer is destroying: the person's body. In the same way, if we genuinely love people, we will hate the thing which, if left unchecked, will destroy the person we love: evil. Again, "Love must be sincere. Hate what is evil; cling to what is good."

So in a sense, love is affirming of the person—as we affirm their value as being made in God's image and as we affirm what's good and true in them. But if it's real love, love does *not* affirm the evil that will destroy them.

LOVE FIGHTS FOR PEOPLE

My friend Bobby Harrington has a great example of how truth in grace saved his father from the alcoholism that could have killed him. Bobby was the lead pastor/minister of the church where both he and his parents served. His dad (Bill) had struggled with alcoholism before coming to faith in his early forties. His repentance had been genuine, and his life was transformed by Jesus.

But after a decade or so, he started to drink again. At first it was when he went out of town, but then it became a regular thing back home.

The men he worked with noticed, including his son-in-law (who also worked with him). His wife, Bobby's mother, tried to talk to him. But nothing reached him. So they decided to follow Jesus' pattern in Matthew 18:15–17:

> If your brother or sister sins, go and point out their fault, just between the two of you. If they listen to you, you have won them over. But if they will not listen, take one or two others along, so that 'every matter may be established by the testimony of two or three witnesses.' If they still refuse to listen, tell it to the church; and if they refuse to listen even to the church, treat them as you would a pagan or a tax collector.

After Bill rejected the input of his wife, as well as his daughter and son-in-law (steps one and two), they asked the leadership of the church to intervene. They asked Bobby to be a part of the intervention because of his good relationship with his dad.

Once the meeting began, Bill got angry. This is typical because Satan brings out our fleshly ways. We find ourselves compelled to protect ourselves from what we perceive as a threat—even when it's meant to rescue us. Yet everyone remained gentle and kind. The conversation focused on how Bill was acting, the harm he was causing to others and himself, and what the Bible taught.

Bill expressed anger again and blurted out something unfair and plainly not true. That made one of the church elders speak up. He literally stuttered as he said, "Now . . . B-B-B-Bill, you know that is not right!" Bill knew this man loved him. For years he had proven his love through kind deeds. He knew what kind of man the elder was. His love was no act.

And when the elder said those stuttering words, Bill changed. Instantly. He slumped in his chair.

"You are right. I know you are right," he said to the elder.

Then he repented. Right there on the spot.

Everyone there helped Bill develop a repentance plan so that he could find true sobriety. The next Monday, Bill went off to a thirty-day treatment program in another city. When he came back, he met with his family to make amends and share the deeper issues he had learned that were driving his alcoholism.

Bill never fell back into alcoholism again. It has been a couple of decades now.

It was genuine love, full of grace *and* truth, that led Bill's family to help him see the error of his ways. Real love clings to what is good and fights what would destroy the person they love. In a world of indifference that poses as "love," it's this kind of *real* love that literally saved Bill's life.

"LOVE IN TRUTH"

In 1 John 3:18, the apostle John helps us with a further clarification on the meaning of *agapaō:* "Dear children," he writes, "let us not love with words or speech but with actions and in truth." The expression "in truth" is important. When we love the way God wants us to love, it happens through actions, not just through words. When we really follow through with action, we show that our love is genuine. It's "in truth," meaning that it's true, authentic love, not just something quick and easy and unproven.

Jesus is the perfect example of love in truth. If anyone proved his love for us through action after action, it was Jesus. The goal of our lives should be to love people the way Jesus loved people. Jesus himself tells us to love others as he loved his disciples: "A new command I give you: Love one another. As I have loved you, so you must love one another. By this everyone will know that you are my disciples, if you love one another" (John 13:34–35).

Let's take a moment and reflect on how Jesus loved his disciples so we can understand as clearly as possible the love we must shift to.

First, when we look at Jesus' example of love as our model, we see how he *loved in truth.* We can clearly see that his love for his disciples was based in reality, not just in words or feelings. Here are seven examples:

- Jesus invested a lot of time in his disciples.
- Jesus was patient with his disciples.
- Jesus upheld God's teachings, even the hard ones, with his disciples.
- Jesus forgave his disciples, even after they had bitterly hurt him (e.g., Peter's denials of knowing Jesus).
- Jesus opened himself up in vulnerable fellowship with his disciples, as in the garden of Gethsemane.
- Jesus rebuked his disciples when they needed it, never affirming sin to gain approval.
- Jesus died on the cross for his disciples, past and present.

The New Testament picture of love places the emphasis not on sentiments or feelings or even words, but on tangible actions. It's true that loveless-yet-sacrificial actions are possible. (Recall Paul's "If I give all I possess to the poor . . . but do not have love" in 1 Corinthians 13:3.) Yet consistently, the picture the New Testament paints of love includes action as the proof that our love goes beyond feelings (which go up and down) and words (which are unreliable and volatile; see James 3:1–12). Again, 1 John 3:18: "Let us not love with words or speech but with actions and in truth."

Second, when we consider Jesus' example, we see that he spoke *truth in love*. He never separated mercy, kindness, and grace from telling them the truth. He was constantly helping his disciples grow by telling them the truth they needed to hear. One of the best ways to summarize what Jesus showed his disciples, as he loved them, is that he was full of both grace *and* truth. The Gospel of John teaches us that this is a good summary of what Jesus was like: "The Word became flesh and made his dwelling among us. We have seen his glory, the glory of the one and only Son, who came from the Father, full of grace and truth" (John 1:14).

Paul writes that speaking the truth to each other in love is how we grow up into Christlikeness: "Speaking the truth in love, we will grow to become in every respect the mature body of him who is the head, that is, Christ" (Ephesians 4:15). Many people have become conditioned to reject any negativity as toxic. Since love involves telling people what they need to hear (instead of just giving them positive vibes), a lot of people are tragically cutting themselves off from love. This is why we must remember that it's not only loving to tell people the truth. We need to make sure we're clearly speaking the truth *in love*, not out of a desire to prove ourselves right.

Thus the New Testament teaches us to focus on Jesus as the perfect example of love. Jesus' life of love can be summarized by the maximum expression of both grace and truth in consistent action to glorify God and help people.

Thus we need to shift our conception of love to loving people regardless of how lovable they are or how sentimental they make us feel. Love, by definition, is not dependent upon how people make us feel. It's driven by a cross-shaped concern to help people and glorify God. This is good and God-honoring, and it's the ultimate sign of what it means to be a disciple of Jesus.

WHEN YOU'RE LOSING THE FIGHT

Relationships that balance work and friendship can hurt.

I understand why I've heard so many times that you can't be friends with someone you lead. It's not easy to pursue friendship when you're also the leader. But if you are the spiritual leader of your home, a leader in the church, or a leader at work, what does this advice leave you with? Perhaps you can decide to be friends only with those who are not in the area where you lead. Maybe an old high school or college friend? Maybe with a leader of a similar function elsewhere? Maybe with someone you share a hobby with? But for most of the hours in your life, what will that leave you with? Friendliness without friendship. Since we were created with a desperate need for real friendship, there will continue to be something major missing.

So my whole ministry career, I have fought the idea that you can't be friends with those you lead. Jesus called his disciples his *friends,* didn't he? Yes, and he is our example.

Yet even Jesus faced disappointment when the friends he discipled did not do well in their role as friends (Matthew 26:40; Luke 22:61). You might think, *He was the perfect disciple maker; what hope do I have?* None—if you expect relationships to be easy! I say this often to myself and to others around our church: We aspire to be mature disciple makers who make mature disciples. That does not mean we are always mature or make mature disciples. We are growing in Christ, yes, but often we have much further to go in our process of sanctification before those we do life with can tolerate the limp we walk with.

Unfortunately, there are times when relationships are failing, even when we have tried our best. They fail because we are both broken. Sometimes we must choose to separate because we just can't figure out how to work through the confusion, the sin, the lies. Yes, we are to continue to love as an act of the will, but sometimes there is just

> **THERE ARE TIMES WHEN RELATIONSHIPS ARE FAILING, EVEN WHEN WE HAVE TRIED OUR BEST.**

so much dysfunction for a variety of reasons. At this juncture, we must make a choice.

What does the enemy want me to do with this situation? I know he wants to isolate me. He wants to make me bitter. He wants me to shift my focus away from what God said in his Word and focus instead on my own feelings of betrayal or disappointment. So what do I do? I could say to myself, *No more! I will not be friends with those I lead. I will choose to stay in my office where no one can hurt me. I will step back from honest relationships because people can't be trusted with the real me.*

Or . . . I can choose to do my best to restore the relationship if I can—as much as it depends on me to live at peace with whoever has hurt me (Romans 12:18). If I have wronged the person, I can do my best to make things right, respect their right to put limits on our relationship as well, and honor those limits. I can listen for the parts of the problem I need to own, confess it, and resolve to do better with the Lord's help. I can choose to fixate less on the ones who hurt me and remember more the ones who didn't. (Admittedly, I tend to overfocus on the few at the expense of the other relationships that God has given me.)

And yes, sometimes I do have to step back from a relationship because it has become unsafe. I may need to remember that everyone fails (especially me), and I may need to forgive them but set boundaries for friendship that they may have never encountered. (Remember, most people have not been discipled, so they only pass on what they have learned from life, which is often not good). Perhaps they have not heeded a scriptural understanding of friendship, though we have addressed it several times in our church.

But God's will for me is not to hate. Or to gossip. Rather, I pray for their well-being even if we have to step back from the relationship.

Navigating friendships as a leader can be hard because those you lead often do not understand the difference between the boss hat and the friend hat. As a leader, you may need to challenge them or even demand better behavior. You may need to make decisions for the good of the team when your team is struggling to see the big picture. Sometimes people can feel that friendship entitles them to having a bigger voice in the decision-making process. Not everyone can handle the distinction between leader and friend, but, for the sake of the organization and the friendship, it does need to be made.

Will such relationships always work? No. Again, life is messy. Has it always worked for me? No. But I could not imagine my life without the friends I still have. I grieve over the losses for sure, but I am so thankful for the wins.

SOME IDEAS FOR MOVING BEYOND MERE FRIENDLINESS

Considering the difficulties we just talked about, it's easy to see why so many leaders opt for friendliness without taking steps toward genuine love and friendship. But as I said earlier, love isn't just an optional add-on for disciples of Jesus. In the final verse of 1 Corinthians 13, Paul says that love, which he has just defined as action guided by patience, kindness, perseverance, etc., is the greatest of the virtues (1 Corinthians 13:13). If we miss this, "discipleship" becomes nothing more than a trendy program.

Not long ago, I met with a pastor who was visiting our church. He approached me after the service, eyes wide. His relatives are a part of our church, and they had recommended our church to him for years. Finally here, he and his wife wanted to check it out and even began attending a life group. He had a million questions for me, and he started the conversation telling me something that didn't seem flattering. But I loved it.

He told me, "I've heard better sermons on relationship. But that isn't what has my attention. I have heard for years how this church reaches the community and how people are getting saved." (We had nine baptisms that weekend, and he got to see some of them.) He continued, "To learn about all the ministries people are serving in together, and then to see it at the life group level all tied together—this blows my mind! How has all this happened?"

My answer was simple: "We try to make mature disciples in relationship." I explained how we grow together to serve together so that people experience relationship with a purpose. It's like a car engine with all its many parts. If you don't add oil, the parts grind against each other and things get hot. That's how fires start and parts wear out. The Holy Spirit moves us to love each other, and that love keeps us living in harmony with each other as we each do our part. Love is worth fighting for because without it, we'll be constantly fighting with each other.

> **WE GROW TOGETHER TO SERVE TOGETHER SO THAT PEOPLE EXPERIENCE RELATIONSHIP WITH A PURPOSE.**

This conversation led to more conversations, and eventually this pastor joined one of our DiscipleShift trainings. Over the years, his church made shifts that helped it more like the biblical church we see in Acts. Here are a few of the steps we encouraged his church to take:

1. Define love in specifics and spiritual maturity in general. What is real biblical love, and what actions are required to show that we love each other, beyond just intellectual ideas?
2. Organize your lives around love behaviors, not just ideas. Funnel everyone into a group where relationship with a purpose is lived out. Make sure you're doing this yourself, since you cannot ask others to do what you won't. In these groups, be intentional about meeting real needs.
3. Celebrate what you want to see practiced. What happens consistently and is celebrated is what creates a culture. Positive peer pressure moves people to the creation of a culture that acts in loving ways. What people see in action will be repeated.
4. Elevate people into leadership who live out this multiplication. Give visible roles to the kinds of people you want to see reproduced. It's easy to recognize and promote the individuals who are gifted in talking about it. You don't want to celebrate those who can merely talk but those who live out what maturity looks like.
5. Take time for this. Knowing each other authentically and helping each other practically take time. Too many surface things that take time away from going deeper and loving more deeply in action are a distraction.

TROUBLED WATER BELOW THE SURFACE

We cannot make it on our own. We need each other. We need to experience love in actions that express Jesus' grace and truth. These kinds of relationships help give us God's strength for the journey. Bad things happen when we miss the crucial foundations of fellowship and love for each other in Scripture. These are things God intended us to have in our lives for our good and his glory.

See, when God asks us to live our lives in a certain way, it's because he loves us. He knows how he designed us and what you and I need to survive and thrive. With that in mind, let's move ahead to the third shift we need to live and lead from relationship. While genuine fellowship and real love don't come naturally for busy people, theoretically, they should resonate with us. This next shift might not resonate so easily. I'm going to ask you to trade something that feels like security and success for something that feels like vulnerability and risk.

A LOVE AS ACTIONS EXERCISE

Take a closer look at 1 Corinthians 13:4–8 with each other. This will likely be a challenging exercise, but it can really help people get closer to each other and grow in the actions of love. Go through this inventory and score yourself. Then ask one other trusted person from your team to provide 360-degree feedback for you using the actions of love described in 1 Corinthians 13. How do they see you? On a scale of 1 (terrible) to 5 (excellent), seek to provide an accurate score based on what you know about each other. No one will get all fives or all ones.

You are patient.	1	2	3	4	5
You are kind.	1	2	3	4	5
You do not envy.	1	2	3	4	5
You do not boast. You are not proud.	1	2	3	4	5
You do not dishonor others.	1	2	3	4	5
You are not self-seeking.	1	2	3	4	5
You are not easily angered.	1	2	3	4	5
You keep no record of wrongs.	1	2	3	4	5
You do not delight in evil but rejoice with the truth.	1	2	3	4	5
You always protect.	1	2	3	4	5
You always trust.	1	2	3	4	5
You always hope.	1	2	3	4	5
You always persevere.	1	2	3	4	5

SHIFT 3

From Recognition to Realness

5

THE RISK OF REALNESS

In the book's introduction, I mentioned that I did not like some of what I was hearing from the people across the country who had read one of my books or been through one of our trainings. Here was the problem: Many were missing that relationship is more than just the context in which discipleship happens. Relationships are more than just a means to an important end.

If you flip to the end of the Bible, you'll see that relationships *are* the end. "Look! God's dwelling place is now among the people, and he will dwell with them. They will be his people, and God himself will be with them and be their God" (Revelation 21:3b).

This is the joy for which Jesus cleared our sins out of the way. Jesus removed the obstacles between us and God so that we can enter a restored relationship with him and, through him, with each other.

So we don't use our time in proximity to people in a utilitarian way—only so that we can teach right doctrine or evangelize. We don't use relational environments only so we can coach people to use their gifts and abilities for Jesus. Yes, these happen. But we were meant to know and love, to be known and be loved. *That's* the life to which he has called us. That's what we desperately need.

And we can shift to regularly fellowshipping with each other and learning to love each other. But without this third shift, we'll hit a ceiling that will prevent us from experiencing the richness of relationships as God intended.

FROM A RECOGNIZED FIGURE TO A REAL PERSON

It can feel good to be recognized as a respected pastor, a great leader, a person of integrity. It feels gratifying to be admired. Sometimes we like this because it feeds our ego. But often, it's just a matter of wanting to be a follower of Jesus who "let[s] your light shine before others, that they may see your good deeds and glorify your Father in heaven" (Matthew 5:16). You want the ministry you're involved in to do well, and it wouldn't help anything if you developed a reputation for having character weaknesses.

This mixed rationale behind wanting to be recognized as a good person explains the risk that surfaces in this third shift: If you get real with people about your needs or flaws, won't that compromise your image and thus cast a shadow on what you're trying to do for God?

And yet Jesus' desire for his disciples is that we are loved *and* known, even as we love and know others (see John 17:20–26). You can't be truly known if you're hiding your true tendencies and weaknesses from the people who could help you. And, for that matter, you can't be truly loved if you're not allowing yourself to be truly known. (They end up loving a cartoon version of the real you.)

I know many who make it their goal to love others no matter what they get in return. They will go visit a person at the hospital the moment they hear there's an emergency, day or night. They will drop what they're doing as soon as they hear someone is hurting or in need of counseling. They are trustworthy and safe for others—but they are still missing something that the Lord wants for all of us.

God wants us to allow others to do the same for us. Fellowship is for all of us. This means we've got to shift our focus from seeking recognition to confessing our realness.

DISCIPLESHIP IS FOR YOU TOO

Believe it or not, living and leading from relationship has several lasting benefits for you as a leader. Consider what benefits the leader receives from getting real and pursuing genuine fellowship as the context for relational discipleship. When leaders allow themselves to be real in relationship, here's what follows:

1. *Less pressure.* When leaders model a culture of realness, it spreads. When everyone in the discipling groups is encouraged to be vulnerable and real, relationships are formed for everyone. The result is pastors not needing to become the relational answer to all the people there. People develop friendships within the group so that the leader is wanted but not needed. The result is that pastors, elders, deacons, and church leaders at every level experience real connections they may not have had.
2. *Met needs.* As people are real with each other, needs are shared, and the church becomes something the people *are* more than just something they *go to*. Church was never meant to be merely a location or an event.

3. *More time.* When people are real with each other, they begin connecting more outside of scheduled gathering times and start serving one another in everyday life as well. They begin to experience real support and accountability from one another, which frees up the pastor to have real relationships as well. Too often pastors try to be everyone else's friend, so they have no time to develop their own real friendships.

4. *More discipleship.* By pursuing realness, leaders are directly modeling for their people something their people can do with others in other contexts to become disciple makers themselves. Most people cannot preach and teach; therefore, what we model on stage in the church is unreproducible for most of our people. If these are the only things we model, we enable them to be spectators whose only job is to invite friends to the show the pastor puts on for the congregation. Our realness removes the spotlight from us and shines it on the one who restores us.

In the previous shift, we focused on what real love looks like. We looked at Paul's writing to the church in Corinth in particular. Paul was dealing with people who had missed the point and needed to learn to love. Where did Paul get the idea that love was the point of all this?

He got it from Jesus. One day Jesus was asked a question that has direct implications for this shift to realness. In that time, teachers of the law regularly discussed which commandments were most important. Traditionally, they had calculated that the Mosaic law held some 613 commandments. All were binding, yet they assumed some commandments were more significant than others. Hence the scribe's question to Jesus:

"Teacher, which is the greatest commandment in the Law?" (Matthew 22:36).

Jesus answered that "all the Law and the Prophets hang on" the commands to love God and other people (Matthew 22:37–41). In other words, everything written in the Old Testament has its basis in *relationship*.

Why would every law point to relationship, you might ask? Well, I believe it is because God knows exactly how he made us and what is best for us. I believe every command is for our good and his glory. And God designed us with relationships in mind; we are literally hardwired for relationships. It's a safe bet to conclude that when these relationships are in place, we are living as God intended and we'll experience joy. In other words, all this talk about relationships and fellowship and love? It's for you too. It's not just to help out your people; it's for your good too.

> **WE ARE LITERALLY HARDWIRED FOR RELATIONSHIPS.**

Yeah, yeah, you might think. *I know.* But do you? Are you prioritizing relationships as if they really are the point to all this? As if they really are God's best for us?

If you're not convinced, I'd encourage you to get there. Because the next thing I'm going to ask you to do could get a little scary if you're on the fence.

LOVE ALWAYS TRUSTS?

Do you remember in 1 Corinthians 13:7 how Paul said that love "always protects, always trusts, always hopes, always perseveres"? In this book's introduction, I shared that the leadership team of a major ministry had told me that they didn't really trust anyone outside of that small room, even as they had hundreds of staff and thousands of volunteer leaders. My response to their statement was, "I thought you told me that you were making disciples here; it sounds like you are making converts. A mature disciple of Jesus is the most trustworthy person there is."

As I see it, there were a couple of problems with the team I was working with. First, discipleship isn't just about teaching doctrine or helping people learn to evangelize, but it's about teaching people to do relationships well. If the teaching and methods in the ministry only deal with Bible knowledge and the vertical relationship and not actual, practical ways of becoming better at person-to-person relationships, then there is something majorly missing from their form of discipleship.

But a second problem had to do with their inability to trust their "disciples." No doubt, they had experienced real hurts, and they were probably just trying not to get burned again. We've all been there, and it's easy to assume there must be something in the Bible along the lines of, "Fool me once, shame on you. Fool me twice . . ."

But what we actually see in Scripture are statements like, "Love always trusts, always hopes, always perseveres."

Real love requires risk for the one doing the disciple making. In the disciple making process, leaders must teach about what real love looks like, and then they must really love. The word for "trusts" in 1 Corinthians 13:7 can mean "believes," "trusts," and "entrusts." Yet it's risky to keep trusting a person. It's scary to entrust myself to another person. It's even harder once they have let me down. But the point of this passage is to describe love as something that keeps giving grace. It keeps forgiving. It keeps fighting for the person. It's a love that *perseveres.*

Jesus was let down over and over by his disciples, and yet he kept on loving them in spite of it. For those of us who are leaders, this means we must entrust ourselves at some level to those we disciple by letting them interact with the real us. We are setting the tone for a new kind of relationship the world has learned to shy away from. In this new kind of relationship, we continue to love even after we are hurt.

When we drop our defensiveness and share what is really happening inside our hearts, it opens doors in others as well. Obviously, this is risky and can and will lead to hurt. This is why we are also told that love keeps no record of wrongs (1 Corinthians 13:5). In our broken world, people fail, intentionally and unintentionally. Again, Jesus dealt with friends who deserted him when they were needed most, and yet, after his resurrection, he returned to them and resumed discipling them. When Jesus told Peter that he should forgive seventy times seven (Matthew 18:22), he was just asking Peter to do the same thing he does with us. What he did even with Judas, who would betray him.

The journey of discipleship is a road that entails both ups and downs. Sometimes we trust and are disappointed, and we may consider withholding trust next time. But then we remember that love is so much more than words and feelings; it's showing patience, kindness, forgiveness, etc. again and again and again. After all, the best discipling lessons taught and learned come through failure and the teaching that comes as a result. Those we disciple learn to forgive well because they have seen us forgive them well.

If we are to be people who truly connect, then we must lead the way. Confront in love when we are hurt, work it out, teach again what is expected in healthy relationships, and then trust again. In those relationships, it's tempting to shy back when the relationship hits a speed bump of disappointment. But you'll find most times that when you make it past the threshold of disappointment and on over into forgiveness and grace, the relationship becomes all the more real and valuable, as you know each other better and love each other more genuinely. Over time in discipling relationships, we truly connect the longer we continue in the process of becoming mature.

RULES FOR RELATIONSHIPS

We all have rules for relationships that we have acquired over time. These rules are created by the teaching we have received, as well as painful experiences we have dealt with. If written out, you would be surprised how different one person's rules are from the next. Many have mainly experienced broken relationships in this world, and that has taught them to take on a form of relationships meant mainly to protect or control. Some just decide to isolate because trying to protect or control doesn't work for long.

As disciple makers, we are to teach people to have Jesus' view of relationships, and to do that we must model it. Jesus' version is filled with risk and forgiveness. When someone fails us (and they will), we trust again because we have hope that they, with the Lord's help, can change. We persevere because Jesus perseveres with us.

This probably means tweaking some of our deep-seated relationship rules.

I am not saying there are no boundaries or that we should trust everyone to the same level. The nuances of this are many and can be complicated, but as mature disciples, we are looking at people as *prospects* needing Jesus and not *suspects*. Why? Because Jesus changes us as we abide in him. We were made for honest, vulnerable relationships in a world of mistrust, self-protection, and pride. The way to have what we were made for is to be in relationship with maturing disciples of Jesus.

IT'S NOT JUST THE *LEADER'S* DESIRE FOR RECOGNITION

Are you starting to see the value in shifting from being a recognized figure to a real person? I hope so. But it's not just you and your fellow leaders that need to be convinced. Chances are a lot of people in your church are comfortable with keeping you on your pedestal.

Pastors and leaders who have come to the right conclusions about discipleship and maturity will have some real obstacles to work through in today's Western church. Why? Because people have grown accustomed to certain expectations of the modern church. It must appear a certain way and work a certain way. Leaders must exhaust themselves to preach better sermons, or infuse a church experience with better worship music, or build more comfortable and inviting buildings.

This ends up being a futile pursuit. Because so many Christians have not matured, they are often mostly concerned with their own preferences. This means that while you might hit the mark for one person, you will inevitably miss it for many others. Pastors know that people get bored quickly, so even if they did hit the mark by giving them some fantastic new experience this week, they worry they have to do it again next week in a whole new way or else lose the people they have. The pressure keeps pastors always moving, and because they try to please as many people as they can each week, they have little time for their own relationships.

They're on the path to being admired for their accomplishments—for a season—but not known for who they are. That's a lonely place to be.

The irony is that, because pastors may be perceived as the only safe person in the church, everyone may want a relationship with them. However, most people are immature spiritually; therefore, they don't tend to do relationships well. Since pastors are others-centered, they can care for others' needs even if that means neglecting their own needs and burning out. The pressure to know everyone leaves them unknown and empty of what they personally need. Without life-giving relationships of their own, they become spiritually and emotionally exhausted. The relational effects on the family leave the pastor's home like so many others—without real relationships.

Success in a church for a disciple maker doesn't equate to gathering a crowd to be entertained or even a group of people to feed. Rather, success translates into growing the number of mature disciples who know the Word and obey it to the point that their relationships with God and others are flourishing. Growing the number of mature disciples takes time and intentionality. But in the end, a movement starts because the people in the church are living the life that God intended. Those outside the church notice that kind of change. To get there, church leaders need to value—and lead their church to value—realness over name recognition.

RELATIONAL ROCK-SKIPPING AND ISOLATION

Here in northern Idaho, it is said we have fifty lakes within fifty miles (we have a lot). Rock skipping becomes an art form here. You probably have done it before, so you know that when you skip a rock, you are trying to throw it as hard as you can at top speed at the top of the water in hopes that it skips along as many times as possible before it sinks.

This is not a bad picture of the relational life of most church leaders (and most Christians in general). People are so busy that they are moving too fast to do anything but skip along the surface of life. We will bounce around with so many people, keeping our conversations light—talking about politics, sports, our kids' activities, and our work. But we never take things too deep or personal. People tend to like us, perhaps because we are friendly or polite or funny, but no one really knows our struggles, our worries, our failures.

I was talking to my son Christian about this, and he coined the phrase "disguised isolation." When he was far from God, he was the life of the party, but no one really knew him. He didn't think he could trust them, and he was right. He thought they would judge him if they knew the truth, so he kept what was really going on inside to himself.

There are many relational rock skippers in the church. Leaders are always starting new ministries; or talking about theology; or discussing philosophies, politics, or the downward spiral of America. They can do all these yet never once talk about their own struggles, weaknesses, or failings. Even when they talk about their own struggles, they typically frame it into a weakness or failing they *used to* have when they were less mature. The recognized figure is still visible and intact; the real person is still safely hidden away.

Pastors and church leaders often absorb the idea that if they were to share their current spiritual struggles with those in their church, they would lose their credibility to lead and shepherd others. They are supposed to be the fix-it guy, not the one that needs fixing! So if they ever get real, they opt for honesty and prayer with pastors from other churches (if they have open interactions at all) because they are afraid to be real with those in their own life.

I think this is misguided and places pastors in a dangerous situation.

IF JESUS SHARED HIS STRUGGLES...

As I mentioned earlier, the perfect Son of God himself shared his inner struggles with the people closest to him (e.g., Matthew 26:36–46). He asked them to stay close, stay awake, and pray during an intensely dark time. He confided in them in this time that his soul was overwhelmed with sorrow, and he didn't want to be left alone. He then cried out to God, asking him to take away his suffering. All the while, he was sweating profusely what looked like drops of blood, a fact some of them had to have witnessed because they wrote about it for us.

Relationship means that we are honest and allow others into our struggle. To be in relationships means they get to love and support us too. Whatever your relational rules have been, *that* ought to take its place toward the top. If you feel that being real with your needs is beneath your position, don't forget that this was a relational norm Jesus himself modeled.

It's true that, in the moment, Jesus did not deal with many of the kinds of things we deal with. He did not deal with lustful thoughts or the enticement of past overcome addictions. However, what he did struggle with he shared for his own good, as well as to be a model his disciples could follow. For many of us who lead, we have had to struggle with things that are both sinful and embarrassing if divulged. The enemy uses that fear and pride to keep us isolated to our demise.

Those in recovery often use a statement that I find helpful here. The expression is this: "We are only as sick as our secrets." The devil's goal is to isolate Christians, especially Christian leaders, in their shame over sin. Like Adam and Eve in Genesis 3, we hide our sin, cover it up, get irritable, and blame others. God wants us to know forgiveness and the freedom it brings. Instead of withdrawing from others to protect our shame and secrets, it is best to share them with the people with whom we experience deep fellowship and love. The devil doesn't want us to love each other in the light of Jesus' grace and truth. He wants us ashamed and to stay hidden in the dark. Scripture teaches us to admit our sins: "Therefore confess your sins to each other and pray for each other so that you may be healed" (James 5:16a).

REALNESS, NOT RECKLESSNESS

We have probably all known people hurt by honesty, so I want to be clear here. I am not advocating that church leaders always share their inner struggles with everyone in their church. Certainly, we must be discerning and prayerful as we decide whom to share with and how to share what is happening within us. We must avoid both spiritual isolation and reckless vulnerability. Handling such matters unwisely can cause us and our family pain and hurt the walk of some who are too immature to handle what we share. So here are some thoughts to consider.

Foster the kinds of relationships that create a culture of honesty. A culture of honesty in the church can keep us from going too far down the road to sin in the first place. In many cases, proactive honesty keeps us from reactionary crises. As leaders, we promote an honest culture when we are appropriately candid in our interactions with the church as a whole (such as during our preaching and teaching times).

FOSTER THE KINDS OF RELATIONSHIPS THAT CREATE A CULTURE OF HONESTY.

Develop deep and lasting relationships with mature people in the church. There are people in our church who are mature enough to handle our deepest issues. They can help us work through shame and pride. In these kinds of bonds, accountability is created. These relationships require discernment and intentionality.

Develop biblical rules with close friends that clarify how to handle our times of struggle. Most Christians have not been discipled on how to be a friend, so this, too, is a part of intentional disciple making. We must take on this issue as leaders, show people what Scripture teaches as the essence of true relationship, and then model it for them. When it comes to our closest, most trusted friends, we need to get very real, and for this realness not to turn into recklessness, it's helpful to have some rules. Here are some examples of rules that have helped me. They are not meant to be exhaustive but are helpful as a starting point:

- If I share something with you, you must not share it with anyone else, unless I am causing harm to myself, my family, or the church.
- By "harm," I mean that I have put myself, my family, or our church in danger legally, or have put my ministry at risk of losing its voice for the Lord.

- If you decide I am not listening and you feel you need to get outside counsel on how to handle this beyond the two of us, you must tell me before you do anything else. There must be no surprises.
- If you decide you need counsel to know how to handle this, then we must decide together who that outside counsel will be.

Enlist a professional Christian counselor help us work through certain seasons. This includes times of spiritual dryness, as well as success. Why seasons of success? I firmly believe success can be more dangerous to our souls than times of trial. There are times when we need more guidance than what an untrained good friend can offer.

I also have found that we need relationships with professional counselors who will help people in our life groups through various issues. Americans are currently suffering through mental health issues of all kinds. So we may need professional help. If someone has a serious mental health issue in one of our life groups, it greatly helps the leader if a professional can provide guidance on how to best love this person through the difficulties. For example, someone struggling with a borderline personality disorder will experience great difficulties when someone challenges their lifestyle. Leading someone with mental health issues requires wisdom, careful guidance, and clear boundaries. Don't be afraid to get help from godly professionals.

Be willing to step down in extreme situations. In extreme situations—such as actively and habitually participating in pornography or falling back into addiction or an affair—we need to be willing to step down from our roles for our own good and for the good of the church. The Bible teaches we all struggle with sin: "We all stumble in many ways" (James 3:2a). But sins that are deliberate and ongoing require a different level of accountability. Hebrews 10 describes them this way:

> If we deliberately keep on sinning after we have received
> the knowledge of the truth, no sacrifice for sins is
> left, but only a fearful expectation of judgment and
> of raging fire that will consume the enemies of God.
> (Hebrews 10:26–27)

For example, a leader who stumbled and looked at pornography and is repentant is in a different place from a leader whose life revolves around an addiction to pornography. Transparency is essential because we can help each other before things get too bad. Don't be fooled: pornography is serious and progressive, and, if left undealt with, it will bring you down. We have an enemy who will make sure of that. We need to practice honest confession to our brothers and sisters. If the sin is gaining power, don't deal with it in isolation. Get help from your brothers and sisters and even professionals before it gets too bad.

Sometimes, however, a sin has been deliberate and ongoing, and a change in leadership is appropriate. God will not bless a church led by a person who is not qualified for the role by ongoing, deliberate, and rebellious secret sin. The enemy will lie to us that we are nothing if we don't have our role. So we can tend to hide things for a while, but this ability will not last for long. The enemy will bring it out when it can do the Lord's reputation and us the most harm.

Real repentance means going past our fear and pride to bring our sin into the light and undergo the consequences with help from the Lord and his people. Godly repentance allows our friends to remember and remind us that our identity is not that we are a pastor or leader, but rather that we are children of God, first and foremost. Again, depending on the sin, we may need to step down or take a break from a leadership position because we have fallen into something that has disqualified us from a leadership role, at least for a time. Our friends can help us walk this out and remind us that we can trust God to love us and provide for us as we begin the confession and repentance stage of our recovery. Remember that if we have godly, honest relationships to begin with, they can keep us from these kinds of situations. The enemy will attack us with shame and fear during this kind of situation, and we need godly friends to help us walk through it to restoration.

WHEN GOD'S CHURCH WAS JESUS TO ME

I'm reflecting on notes I wrote going through a dark season in my family. The notes are several years old, and my son is now serving the Lord, but I think my reflections from this time in my story will help illustrate my point that *we need realness* with each other or we're not going to make it.

> *Right now, my adult son Christian is at a treatment center for anxiety, depression, and constant paranoid thoughts. He is a Christian now and is walking with the Lord and with fellow Christians in relationship, but in earlier years, he was far from the Lord and was a drug addict. We went through two treatment programs with him, and he finally spent time in a homeless shelter. He eventually surrendered his life to Jesus and got sober. He is now married to a wonderful woman and has a brand new child. While he was far from God, he had fathered*

another child and, once sober, he has also taken responsibility to be the father God wanted him to be with this child as well.

As you might expect, in the years after gaining sobriety, Christian did the hard work of rebuilding, and it wasn't easy. I am so proud of him. Over time, he became a youth minister. He was doing so well in that role. But in the last six months, he has been struggling with anxiety in profound ways. A major part of the problem is the damage done to his brain while he was on drugs has had a long-term effect. (Our past sin can leave lingering consequences that we must deal with even years later.) Currently, doctors are trying to regulate his medications, a process that can take a while.

Christian phones me every night from his treatment center. He's very honest with me, and he can't wait to share what he's been thinking throughout each day. Sometimes he feels trapped in lies that the enemy, and his broken mind, whispers in his ear. The conversation with me helps him get unstuck. For instance, the devil tries to tell him he's the only one to ever struggle like this. But as we talk things out, he realizes that he is not alone; many people (including me) have felt the way he feels.

The other day, he felt so far away from God and unworthy. He doubted God because of his situation. As we talked through his honest doubts, I was able to just listen so he could get it out into the light. I was then able to remind him of ways God had saved him from death many times. We were able to remember together all the ways the Lord had loved him. I was able to go to Scripture with him and bolster his understanding of where God is even in times of darkness.

One of my pastor friends is near where Christian is staying and visits him. Together, they speak about his struggles. This friend listens, cries with him, prays for him, and shares his own common struggles, and I can see Christian gain strength from his time with this man. Each time we talk, I can sense his head clearing. I can help right now because, in all honesty, I am being helped with my own struggles with God.

I must confess that I have been, and still am at times, angry at God. My wife and I prayed every day for years that God would save our son from his addiction and keep him safe even when he was in the homeless shelter alone. God answered us, and my son gave his life to the Lord. We have seen the profound way the Lord is now using him in the lives of others. Yet now all those things that he did years ago, the consequences of past actions, are flooding back into his life out of nowhere. I don't understand God right now! Why would he save Christian when he was in a drug-induced coma . . .? Why would he save him from a life of jail and crime . . .? Why would he save him when he was in the homeless shelter . . . only now—after he has been changed—to allow him to lose his mind like this?

Even as I am talking to Christian to encourage him, I am feeling anger and doubt. I am so blessed that I can cry out to God and say to him, "I believe; help me in my unbelief." And he hears me. I am so grateful that I can honestly write this here and know that I will not be fired by my leaders in the church because I have doubts and anger. I am so grateful that I have people in my life that support Lori (my wife) and my other boys, Jesse and Will. I am so thankful that I have been able to honestly talk to the elders in my church and the staff. They didn't judge me. They didn't punish me with silence so the devil could fill in the blanks with lies that would further isolate me. They prayed for me, and they reached out to my son's wife. I am so thankful for my life group and men's groups of *regular believers who have allowed me to be honest and constantly pray for me.*

I don't know how I would make it if I did not have brothers and sisters who help carry my burdens when I am so tired.[4]

Now years later, looking back at what I wrote then, I am more convinced than ever that living a life of realness is vital. Transparency and vulnerability were key not only for my son but for me; it is key for all of us. We all need to be connected with other believers so we can share what we're struggling with, confess our doubts and sins, and pray for one another so we can do life together. This is how God intended us to live, even through difficult times.

And if we look, we'll see people in the Bible going through similar heartache and confusion: David's psalms of confusion and fear; Elijah's despair and readiness to give up and die; John the Baptist's doubts about Jesus while in jail. We need to love, yes, but we need to allow others to know and love us too. In fact, when you as a leader are honest about who you really are, others will come out of hiding and be honest too.

If we want to make it as leaders, the risk of realness is worth it.

But what if we're not so concerned about our own health as leaders—we're mainly just trying to get our church from A to B? In that case, isn't a lot of what we're talking about in this book a distraction from getting things done? That's the question we explore in the next chapter.

6

A TO B

T he principles described in this book probably sound right: *Fellowship. Love as a cross-shaped action. Realness.* But they're going to be easy to forget when you put down this book and get hit with the next deadline.

This is because, at the end of the day, perhaps you believe that as nice as these things are in theory, they aren't what it takes to lead a church. Maybe you, like many other leaders, believe deep down that shifts like these might have worked for you in a different life. And hopefully they can take root in other people in your church. But when it comes to the life you're living, with its urgent demands and influential tasks, you might think you probably will need to keep skipping rocks when it comes to relationships—so you can do what it takes to get your church from Point A to Point B.

In other words, perhaps at the root, you really do think your church needs the recognized figure more than the real person. Your gut tells you that the recognized figure is the person who can truly take this ministry where it needs to go.

You're not trying to be prideful. In fact, you're very aware of your personal weaknesses, and you'd like to be better with relationships and all that. But you've got a ministry to lead. Staff to hire. Volunteers to train. Sermons to write. Fires to extinguish. Unsaved people to bring to Christ. All this means hours you don't really have to do a job you can't really do, even as you give it your best shot. So yeah, maybe in another life, you could add in the deep relationship stuff too. But you're living *this* life, not some other one, and you've got to get your church from A to B.

A MONARCH WOULD UNDERSTAND, RIGHT?

If anyone should understand the need to do what it takes to get from A to B, it's a king. So let's pause and consult one. We're in luck because the one we'll get to hear from was famously blessed with an impressive gift of wisdom. His name was King Solomon.

Solomon was the main voice behind three Old Testament books: Proverbs, Song of Songs, and Ecclesiastes. Ecclesiastes is noteworthy in being so incredibly realistic about the futility of the human condition without God.

In Ecclesiastes 4, Solomon is also realistic about where the path described at the beginning of this chapter will take you.

Starting in Ecclesiastes 4:8 and moving through verse 12, Solomon describes the person who neglects relationships to get from A to B. Interestingly, with as much wisdom as Solomon was entrusted with, he often squandered it and acted foolishly. His own foolish decisions along the way seem to provide the backdrop for much of the descriptions of futility in Ecclesiastes. Solomon proves that it is entirely possible to be a part of God's chosen people and reject the wisdom God gives you. Throughout Solomon's experiments with foolish behaviors, he discovered some hard-earned *aha* moments. He seems to be describing one of them right here, and it echoes what we have been writing about in this book.

> There was a man all alone;
>> he had neither son nor brother.
> There was no end to his toil,
>> yet his eyes were not content with his wealth.
> "For whom am I toiling," he asked,
>> "and why am I depriving myself of enjoyment?"
> This too is meaningless—
>> a miserable business! (Ecclesiastes 4:8)

Notice the man he is writing about is without family or friends, and all he does is work, work, work. He apparently has plenty to do, and one result of all his hard work is that he's grown wealthy. But his work lacks meaning and he's unhappy. He's become unclear about why he is working so hard—he has no one to share his wealth with. Oh, he has plenty of people around, but he feels that he is absolutely alone.

You can have people around, be successful in your job, and yet be totally isolated, which leads to emptiness.

AT LEAST WE'RE MOVING FROM A TO B, RIGHT?

We may think that our relationally depleted productivity is at least getting us somewhere. I suppose it is, but it's nowhere good. More addiction. More divorce. More suicides. As I ponder this subject, sadly I am hearing more and more about pastors who take the route of suicide or at least attempt it. Our young people are following suit, here in the most prosperous country in the world. Around here, we have had so many teen suicides (mostly from middle-class families) that a special project had to be created called "Irreplaceable." Our church recently partnered with the local school district and mental health professionals in our area to work on this project. In it we deal with the lies these kids believe that would lead them to attempt or commit death by suicide.[5] In the United States, there are, on average, 130 suicides per day, with the rate highest in middle-aged men.[6]

There are many different reasons for these tragic facts. A major reason is the truth that, just as it was three thousand years ago when Solomon wrote Ecclesiastes, life without real relationship is empty.

According to one study, some two in five pastors have seriously considered leaving ministry. Their top reasons? Number one is the high level of stress in the job, and number two is feeling lonely and isolated.[7] You might assume that those pastors must be the ones that are not very successful, but you would be wrong. Many have large and growing churches that show all the outward signs of success in numbers. However, many pastors feel such great pressure to succeed because their identity in their own eyes is based on success in other people's eyes, often in the eyes of other pastors. So often, pastor gatherings can become contests for whose church is growing the most.

So you are either driven to do better to compete, or you're discouraged because you're not succeeding in the way success is defined in our culture. You end up wanting to give up, or because of jealousy and resentment, you badmouth those who are seemingly successful so that you don't look so bad. Some think, and even may say things like, *They are growing because they compromised the truth.* There may be some who have, but often the real reason we are irritated is because we don't see our faithful work being rewarded with the book deal, or the speaking role from up front at the conferences we attend.

Other pastors and leaders are there looking for the quick fix that will set them off toward success in the pastoral world, and they are ready to do almost anything to win. There are plenty of great pastors who don't get caught up in all of that, but far too many do. For those who do, the amount of work they are willing to keep doing when they get home is unhealthy. It causes a ripple effect in their time of spiritually abiding in Christ. They do so much work *for* God (but also for themselves and for their drive to succeed), that they don't spend real time *with* God. They are exhausted from their work so that when they do get a day off, it's a recuperation day to rest up and then return and get back to doing what's "important" at work. Who pays for this?

The ones who are most taxed end up being what should have been their first responsibility: their family. Ironically, these are the ones they likely say they care about the most. This leads to a life of disguised isolation, which can often lead you to physical isolation. Church leaders and their spouses become vulnerable to things that might look like escape, for example, addiction or an affair. Rather than escaping, they only find themselves in a new kind of dungeon.

But at least we're still moving our church from A to B, right?

Solomon would say no. In Ecclesiastes 4, the king continues by describing how much better it is to do life in relationship. Don't miss that he's not just saying better = more fulfilled; or that better = more spiritual. He's saying that life together = better = more A to B:

> Two are better than one,
> > because they have a good return for their labor:
> If either of them falls down,
> > one can help the other up.
> But pity anyone who falls
> > and has no one to help them up.
> Also, if two lie down together, they will keep warm.
> > But how can one keep warm alone?
> Though one may be overpowered,
> > two can defend themselves.
> A cord of three strands is not quickly broken.
> > (Ecclesiastes 4:9–12)

We all know that "two are better than one" spiritually or theoretically. But practically? Yep. Consider some observations:

- With two, there can be another set of eyes to see from different perspectives. Multiple views make for better ideas and more solutions.
- With two, we double our speed and compound our strength.
- With two, not only do we get more work done and do it faster, but the shared wisdom makes for better planning so that the right work is done in the first place.
- With two, doing work together keeps pride from taking over in the life of an individual. So often, when the work is done by an individual, they alone are given the credit. It's easier to handle the load of success when it is shared.

We've got to get this. Relationships aren't a distraction from the point. They are inextricable from the point. They don't slow us down from getting from A to B. In fact, without relationships, is there even a B to get to?

IF ANYBODY HAD AN EXCUSE TO SKIP ROCKS

If any of us church leaders feel especially productive in our ministries, there's a quick way to reverse that opinion of ourselves: read about Paul in the book of Acts. He's hopping from city to city, country to country, even continent to continent, all to spread the gospel to as many people as possible in his lifetime. If anybody had reason to set aside relational depth for ministry productivity, it was Paul.

It's instructive that his longest tenure we read about was only three years. For him, that was a long time in one place. Then he was off again to plant another church because he only had so many years and there was so much work to do. On his way to Jerusalem, Paul happened back through the area and, though he was in a hurry to reach Jerusalem by the festival of Pentecost, he wanted to connect with the Ephesian elders for what would likely be the last time. If you've read the rest of Acts, you know that in Jerusalem he would be arrested and jailed for a couple years. While there, he would appeal to be tried before Caesar, and, as a result, he would go as a prisoner aboard a ship to Rome. With Paul in Rome, the book of Acts ends.

Now, here's the deal. Paul knew that he would be leaving this young Ephesian church someday. And if he had any sense, don't you think that Paul would have been smart enough not to get too close? When you get too close, it can hurt when you have to leave. But apparently Paul hadn't thought that through because as Paul was telling the Ephesian church leaders goodbye for the last time . . . it was like the emotional last night of church camp.

> When Paul had finished speaking, he knelt down with all of them and prayed. They all wept as they embraced him and kissed him. What grieved them most was his statement that they would never see his face again. Then they accompanied him to the ship. (Acts 20:36–38)

You read that and get the feeling that this is no ordinary church. This isn't the typical church where you come and you sit and you sing and you listen—and then go home and do your own thing throughout the week. Somehow this band of believers in Ephesus really connected. How did they connect so deeply? Acts 20 gives us a couple clues as to how this church did it.

TEARS AND TRUTH

The first clue as to how the Ephesian church had bonded so closely is mentioned three times in this passage where Paul meets with them for the last time:

> When they arrived, [Paul] said to them: "You know how I lived the whole time I was with you, from the first day I came into the province of Asia. I served the Lord with great humility and with *tears* and in the midst of severe testing by the plots of my Jewish opponents." (Acts 20:18–19)

> So be on your guard! Remember that for three years I never stopped warning each of you night and day with *tears*. (Acts 20:31)

> They all *wept* as they embraced him and kissed him.
> What grieved them most was his statement that they
> would never see his face again. (Acts 20:37–38a)

The first clue as to how this church connected so deeply is the
word "tears." Here's the second clue:

> You know that I *have not hesitated to preach anything that
> would be helpful* to you but have taught you publicly and
> from house to house. I have declared to both Jews and
> Greeks that they *must turn to God in repentance* and have
> faith in our Lord Jesus. (Acts 20:20–21)

> Now I know that none of you among whom I have gone
> about preaching the kingdom will ever see me again.
> Therefore, I declare to you today that I am innocent of the
> blood of any of you. For I have not hesitated to *proclaim to
> you the whole will of God.* (Acts 20:25–27)

The second clue as to how this church connected so deeply is called "truth." Paul kept telling them the truth, over and
over. And notice it was the *whole* truth. He didn't shrink back
from telling them "anything that would be helpful" and "the
whole will of God." Paul was telling them the truth, the whole
truth—not just what people wanted to hear, not just what their
culture said was okay.

Why did Paul get so involved in the relational lives and
spiritual outcomes of the people when he knew he would soon
be moving on to more and more churches? It's because relationships aren't beside the point. They don't distract from the A to
B we need to get our churches to. Discipling people into Christlikeness and his mission *is* the destination. Paul described

people in the church as "my dear children, for whom I am again in the pains of childbirth until Christ is formed in you" (Galatians 4:19).

> DISCIPLING PEOPLE INTO CHRISTLIKENESS AND HIS MISSION IS THE DESTINATION.

WELL, THAT'S ONE WAY TO DO CHURCH

How do tears and truth connect people so deeply? It's because it was tears and truth joined *in relationship*. They spent time together. Paul was connecting with them "publicly *and* from house to house" (Acts 20:20). They were in each other's homes, learning the truth together, and crying tears together.

It's easy to look at that and think, *Well, that's one way to do church, but can't we just do church the ordinary way? You know, where Sunday comes around, and you come and sit and sing and listen and then leave?* It would seem that, with such an easy bar to clear, churches could grow faster and more efficiently get from A to B.

We can even work that logic into our sales pitch for getting someone to come to church. Imagine the following conversation:

"I don't think I really want to start going to church. I don't think I can really do the church thing."

"Well, why not?"

"Well, I just don't have the kind of time, for one thing. I've already got a very full schedule. And I've already got enough of a social life. I just don't think I have time to do the church thing."

"Oh, don't worry about time! It's just Sunday morning. It just takes an hour on Sunday mornings. And really, most people come half the time anyway; it's not a big deal. I mean, there are small groups and stuff like that, but you don't really have to worry about that. Doing the church thing can actually be really easy. It doesn't have to really demand much from you."

It's like we're convincing a Baby Boomer to go ahead and get a smartphone:

"I am not getting one of those smartphones."

"Well, why not?"

"Well, I'll tell you. My phone bill is already way too much, and I'm not about to double my phone bill."

"Oh, well, a smartphone doesn't have to double your phone bill. In fact, I know of companies that can get you a data plan with a smartphone, and the monthly bill is half of what you're paying right now. Going with a smartphone could mean fewer telemarketer calls and paying less for the plan."

"Oh, I didn't know that."

Here's how this kind of reasoning goes:

"But, if I go ahead and sign up for such-and-such, I'll have to do such-and-such. And I don't have time or interest in doing that."

"No, no, no—you don't have to do such-and-such. You can still sign up without having to do such-and-such."

"You're saying I can sign up without having to do such-and-such?"

"Yep."

"Well, I might actually think about signing up then."

Back to Paul and the Ephesian elders in Acts 20. That's a church which sheds tears together and speaks truth to each other. They were deeply connected. We tend to look at that and think, *Well, that's one way to do church. But there's just too much I'd have to do if we get too relational. It's better to keep doing church the ordinary way.*

The problem is that we call the cycle of coming, sitting, singing, listening, and leaving "church." We really ought to use a different word. That's not *church*. Church is shedding tears together and speaking truth to each other. Christians need to be telling each other that it matters what they're going through. That's why Christians do tears together. Christians need to be telling each other that it matters what they become. That's why Christians speak truth to each other. Church minus togetherness and realness is something less than *church*.

If you want church minus the togetherness and realness, you might as well be asking, "Now, if I sign up for tennis, I don't have to hit the ball over the net, do I?" Or, "Now, if I go fishing with you, I won't actually have to catch *fish*, will I?"

And yet, we think, *Now, I can do church, but I don't really have to connect with people, do I?* But church happens in togetherness. Without togetherness, you don't have church. That's what you've signed up for. Doing tears and truth together *is* church the ordinary way, according to the Bible.

BUT . . . HAVE YOU SEEN MY SCHEDULE?

We in America often feel that we don't have to bring our realness into church. After all, many of us are already bringing our time and talents. Plus we in America tend to be exceptionally busy; what more does church need from us?

We have shopping to do . . . but then Ephesus also had a huge market in the middle of the city. We have sports to watch when we get home and unplug . . . but then Ephesus had a stadium to watch sporting events, chariot races, and gladiator fights. We have movies to watch . . . but then Ephesus had a theater with a 24,000-seating capacity. We have music to listen to . . . but then Ephesus had its musical events at the festivals. We have sites to visit and vacations to plan . . . but then Ephesus had a temple that was one of the seven wonders of the ancient world.

I know we're busy, but so were those in Ephesus. And still the church at Ephesus was connected. They were doing tears together. They were doing truth together. It was beautiful.

And it moved people from A to B. Imagine that.

SPEEDING THROUGH LIFE AND MISSING IT

The story is told of a boy named Peter who was always bored, always waiting for whatever came next in life.[8] In winter, he longed for summer; in summer, he couldn't wait to go sledding in the snow.

One day, Peter is walking in the forest. An old woman offers him a magic silver ball with a golden thread dangling out of it.

She tells him, "This is your life thread. Do not touch it and time will pass normally. But if you wish time to pass more quickly, you have only to pull the thread a little way and an hour will pass like a second. But I warn you, once the thread has been pulled out, it cannot be pushed back in again. It will disappear like a puff of smoke."

He grabs it out of her hand with a smile.

So Peter gets to school, magic ball in his pocket, and starts feeling bored. He tugs the thread, and suddenly the teacher is telling everyone to get ready to go home. After a few days like this, Peter thinks it will be fun to simply skip to summer break. And you can probably guess what sorts of things happen next. He jumps ahead to graduation. He's ready to get married when a letter comes—he's been drafted to go to war. After the military gets burdensome, he gives the thread a good tug, and he's home with his new wife. They have a baby, and he's able to make the child's fussy nights and seasons of sickness pass in a moment. When times are hard at work, he tugs the thread, and times are better. So much easier, though, when the kids are out of the house, he thinks to himself, and they don't have such a crowded house and tight budget. He tugs, and all the kids are out of the house with their own families. His wife is starting to show her age; she's often ill. It's tough to see her suffer, so another tug.

They're a white-haired couple now, and Peter's had a life without boredom and without pain. Yet Peter realizes that such a life has itself been boring. And he feels a pain of emptiness, like there was something major missing in his life. He realizes that the real gift wasn't a magic ball. The real gift was his lifetime. The problem is, he skimmed through it.

I don't want to pretend like the church is always amazing. That if you just spend more time with church people, you'll always walk away with a smile. No, sometimes we'll annoy each other. That's what family members do to each other sometimes. Church is far from perfect. It's made of us, after all. But the church—warts and

THE CHURCH—WARTS AND ALL—IS THE REAL GIFT.

all—is the real gift. It's God's gift to us, to help us get through. To help us grow up.

You don't want to skim through this gift.

You don't want to get to the point where you look at your life and you realize that, even though you're growing older, you haven't been growing up—because you haven't really been doing *church*. You've been doing something less than church.

It's in getting real with each other and speaking truth to each other that we find ourselves not only growing older together but growing up into something beautiful:

> So Christ himself gave the apostles, the prophets, the evangelists, the pastors and teachers, to equip his people for works of service, so that the body of Christ may be built up until we all reach unity in the faith and in the knowledge of the Son of God and become mature, attaining to the whole measure of the fullness of Christ. Then we will no longer be infants, tossed back and forth by the waves, and blown here and there by every wind of teaching and by the cunning and craftiness of people in their deceitful scheming. Instead, speaking the truth in love, we will grow to become in every respect the mature body of him who is the head, that is, Christ. From him the whole body, joined and held together by every supporting ligament, grows and builds itself up in love, as each part does its work. (Ephesians 4:11–16)

We need to be telling each other that it matters what we're going through; again, that's why Christians do tears together. We need to be telling each other that it matters what we become; that's why Christians do truth together. And it's totally worth it.

If you want to get your church from A to B, don't forget what B actually is.

A RELATIONSHIP GUIDELINES EXERCISE

In Chapter 5, I shared my personal guidelines for relationships as they relate to sharing my struggles with others. Review my list with your team and ask each other if you're willing to adopt these, or similar, guidelines with each other. Perhaps you'll choose to add to them or take away from them. Complete the exercise by coming up with the guidelines you will follow with each other for how you share things, using this list as a starting point:

- If I share something with you, you must not share it with anyone else unless I am causing harm to myself, my family, or the church.
- By "harm," I mean that I have put myself, my family, or our church in danger legally, or have put my ministry at risk of losing its voice for the Lord.
- If you decide I am not listening and you feel you need to get outside counsel on how to handle this beyond the two of us, you must tell me before you do anything else. There must be no surprises.
- If you decide you need counsel to know how to handle this, then we must decide together who that outside counsel will be.

SHIFT
4

From Skeptical to Safe

7

AM I SAFE?

Not long ago, the chairman of our eldership and I were working with another pastor and his eldership team that were in crisis. My elder asked their team, "On a scale of one to ten, what level of trust do you have on your team for one another?" One of their elders said maybe a two, to which everyone agreed. This information was a large indicator to us as to why they found themselves in crisis.

As we were meeting with this team of leaders and sharing the importance of dealing with their lack of trust, their chairman asked John (my elder) what his level of trust was for those on our eldership. He said it could not be higher and went on to explain why. As he talked, I thought of two things. First, I praised God because I felt the same way. Second, I reflected back to just seven years before, when we had gone through a season when John and I would have answered in a much different way.

SKEPTICAL OF EACH OTHER

It was right after the hardest time in many years in my marital life. Lori and I had struggled to stay on the same page as our son lived his life of rebellion and drug addiction. The stress his actions put on my other sons was requiring a great deal of emotional and relational energy. Not only was I exhausted, I was also frustrated with our church. I felt like I had been forced for an extended period of time to become a manager in my position rather than a leader, and it was becoming a real struggle. In part this was due to my situation at home, but it was also because we were having to spend time trying to organize and go deeper with the explosive growth we had encountered for several years in our congregation. With this growth came job changes, administrative issues, skill set inadequacies, and so on. All things I had no training or experience in, so it always felt like we were building the plane while we were flying it. During that time, with the help of the elders and executive team of our church, I decided to take a sabbatical.

The church was fifteen years old, and I had never taken a prolonged rest, so it was time. But it was not what I expected in any way. In the first week of my sabbatical, my wife and I got into a four-wheeler accident, which changed the trajectory of my time off. It was serious enough that I became a stay-at-home nurse for much of my time off. At the same time, I discovered that one of my staff purposely staged a mini coup with ten of our families while I was gone. I had never had this happen before, and it upset me to the core. Loyalty is a big deal to me, and I felt betrayed. Added to that, the leadership team that was in charge while I was gone did not handle it the way I would have liked. When I came back from sabbatical (if you could even call it that), I had to enter into several other messy situations, and that again proved frustrating.

During the time I was away, I had become convinced that we needed to take ground again and move forward. However, the elders were not in agreement; they wanted to keep doubling down on structure and organization. Added to that, they confronted me on some issues they felt I needed to address in my leadership style. They felt I was not listening to them well enough and that I needed to slow down. But in my mind, they did not handle this confrontation the way they should have either.

As things progressed, it became apparent that there wasn't as much trust on the team as I had thought. As we each tried to deal with what had been a low to-medium-level frustration, our time spent away from each other was being used by the enemy to fill the gaps in communication with negative narratives about the other person's motives. Emotional temperatures and frustration started to rise to new levels. This led to me telling my elders and executive team that maybe it was time for me to move on. In fact, I was pretty sure it was.

The elders made it clear they did not want me to leave, but they did think I needed to be willing to slow down and make some changes. Now remember, I was the co-founder of our church, and all of them had come in under my tenure as leader. I felt that I deserved better than this, and I believed these men were not being loyal. I felt betrayed because they had not shared their individual issues with me in a way I understood, and instead they had talked about this collectively with each other. In my mind, this was gossip and a rejection of Matthew 18 on dealing with a brother. When I mentally coupled this situation with the mini-coup event, I felt unsafe and hurt.

WISE WORDS FROM A TRUE FRIEND

While this was all brewing and unresolved, I made a trip overseas. I had previously made a commitment to go to on the trip, and, even though I didn't have time, I needed to follow through on that commitment. As I spent time with the leadership team I was working with on this trip, I shared where I was and asked them to pray about it for me.

That evening the leader of the ministry I was working with, someone I respect very much, came to talk to me about it. He asked me a question that he knew the answer to. Thinking back on it now, I realize he just wanted me to say it out loud. He said, "Jim, I know you are the pastor and part of the eldership on your team. Do you believe that eldership is a part of God's design for his church?"

"Yes," I said.

He asked, "Do you believe in the plurality of eldership?"

I said, "Yes, I believe there should never be one person leading a church. I believe that every individual elder is under the authority of the eldership as a whole."

This led him to ask, "Do you believe that every person needs to be submissive to their delegated authority, unless that authority asks you to sin against God?" Well, I am no idiot, and by now I could see where these questions were going. He then asked me, "Do you think that the elders are asking you to sin?" I reluctantly said no. He asked, "Is it possible that you need to deal with what they are asking you to deal with, rather than hiding behind the way they did it?"

Ouch!

As I reflected on our conversation that night, I came to realize that I had often been teaching submission under delegated authority (Hebrews 13:17). In my mind, being able to submit to leadership and having the quality of humility are proof of spiritual maturity. I had to ask myself, *Is that for everyone or just other people besides me?* I was busted.

TURNING THE TOUGH QUESTIONS ON ME

My friend also spoke about my getting stuck on what made them untrustworthy to me rather than focusing on *what had made me untrustworthy to them*. The way they had done this neither excused nor made irrelevant the fact that they felt I was not safe. They felt they had to talk to others to be able to then come to me, rather than being able to deal with the issues alone with me. This suggested that the way I handled and reacted to things made it hard for others to approach me.

Why was that?

To be honest, I didn't know. *I am totally safe with myself, so why wouldn't they be?* I thought. (When I say that out loud or write it on a page, it sounds so silly to even have that cross my mind.) So I decided to focus on the question, "What makes me untrustworthy to them?" and work on that. That was my part, which was the only part I had control of. God would have to deal with them on their part, and I believed he would. I had to be willing to own my part by faith even when I wasn't sure they would allow God to deal with them.

When I got home from the trip, I went to the elders and shared what the Lord had been teaching me through a trusted brother. I told them that I was not going to leave. I was going to submit to their authority and trust that the Lord was speaking through the whole of the group on whether we moved forward in the ways I had wanted to. I shared with them that I had been hurt, but, rather than share at the time what had hurt me, I had fought in an ungodly way. I asked for forgiveness and then started focusing on the questions that had really hit me hard while I was away: Why didn't these men trust me, and what could I do to change that?

The solution wasn't to continue being skeptical of them, but rather to ask if I was a safe person. That humility began to disarm us all.

And so, as our elder John shared his current level of trust for me and our team with the group we were working with, I reflected on my level of trust as well. I was blown away by the changes God had made in all of us as individuals, but especially in us as a team. So I asked this other eldership team to do what I had to do years before. Rather than start to share what made the others on the team seem untrustworthy to them, I asked them to consider what made them seem untrustworthy to each other. This would mean they would have to ask questions to understand rather than remaining defensive. They would have to forgive the wrongs they perceived had been done to them and seek forgiveness for what they had done, even if it had been unintentional.

FROM SKEPTICAL TO SAFE

As you might have guessed by now, our team prioritizes relationship over strategy when training others. Many books speak to the truth that you can only function as a team at the speed of trust. I would agree and argue it's the same in your marriage and in most areas of our lives. Relationships only go as deep as trust allows. A low trust factor leads to a shallow depth of relationship. For people who were built for deep and authentic relationships, as God created humans, trust really matters. And because the Bible is a book about relationship from start to finish, it has a great deal to say on the subject of trust and trustworthiness.

When I speak or write about trust, I picture several different things I've learned from the Scriptures. If I were to say that you are a trustworthy person, I would be saying that *you are a safe person to be in a relationship with* because I see seven attributes in you. Here are the seven attributes (my "Big 7"[9]) that I look for in someone with whom I am going to have a deep, authentic relationship:

1. *Courage* – You speak the truth in love even when it is hard. You tell me what I need to hear rather than I want to hear. This commitment to truth means I can respect you even if I don't agree with you.
2. *Honesty* – You keep your word. You tell me the truth about yourself. You don't lie.
3. *Humility* – You are coachable. You can admit to being wrong and ask for forgiveness. You can be a servant to the needs of others at the expense of your image.
4. *Loyalty* – You don't gossip. You don't run for cover when it gets hard to be a friend. You keep a confidence when entrusted with it. You defend me to others even if it costs you to do so. You give me the benefit of the doubt when you hear things about me you don't like and will come to me personally to find out.
5. *Wisdom* – Scripture guides your perspective and actions. As someone who desires wisdom, you consider others' perspective when you deal with things or issues they are responsible for or are connected to.
6. *Reconciliation* – You point me and others to God's heart when conflict arises. You seek reconciliation. Your goal is to put out fires rather than put gas on them. You fight for the restoration of relationships.

7. *Forgiveness* – Our relationship will not be easy to break. There is safety in a relationship when you know both people have the right expectations. Even when we fail, we know we will work it out.

I believe that you will find these things consistent with the biblical teachings on trustworthiness. As the living Word, Jesus is the perfect example of trustworthiness, and we are becoming more trustworthy as we follow him.

Some people have low trust for others in general because of past trauma and experiences. They may have had instances where those they trusted were not trustworthy in any sense. Other people have an unrealistic perfectionist bent, where their expectations can never be met so they find themselves trusting no one. Whatever a person's past experiences, the issue of trust has to be dealt with if we are to have deep relationships. Having a clear idea about what trust means for you and agreeing on this with those you are in relationships with can keep misunderstanding from creeping in and dividing you. Part of the maturing process is dealing with the issue of building, maintaining, and repairing trust in relationships. I've found that the first step is a matter of going first in submitting to the tough questions.

> **THE FIRST STEP IS A MATTER OF GOING FIRST IN SUBMITTING TO THE TOUGH QUESTIONS.**

THE BIBLICAL BASIS FOR GOING FIRST

An important verse that comes to mind when I think about the need to ask tough trust questions of myself is 1 John 4:19–21:

> We love because he first loved us. Whoever claims to love God yet hates a brother or sister is a liar. For whoever does not love their brother and sister, whom they have seen, cannot love God, whom they have not seen. And he has given us this command: Anyone who loves God must also love their brother and sister.

Here are some observations from this verse that I think are important:

- We know what love is because God first showed us what it looks like.
- He loved us first and now desires that we love others in the same way.
- If I am to follow his example, I must pursue trustworthiness, show integrity, and go first regardless of what others do.

If you are around our church staff much, you will hear me talk about the idea of integrity a lot. Integrity is very important to me. Years ago, I read something that Jesus said about it, and it has stuck with me ever since. In Matthew 23:2–4, Jesus said to the crowds and to his disciples:

> The teachers of the law and the Pharisees sit in Moses' seat. So, you must be careful to do everything they tell you. But do not do what they do, for they do not practice what they preach. They tie up heavy, cumbersome loads and put them on other people's shoulders, but they themselves are not willing to lift a finger to move them.

Here is what strikes me in this passage. Jesus condemned the Pharisees for what I deem a lack of integrity. Now by that, I don't mean that Jesus was condemning the Pharisees for not being perfect. He knew no human (other than himself) could be. He condemned them because they would not practice what they taught. More than that, they made the law so much more burdensome than it was intended to be and would not help others carry it. As Jesus' disciples today, we cannot be perfect, but we must sincerely live out what we teach others to live out. We cannot command others to do what we are not putting effort toward doing.

So when I am thinking about trustworthiness and all that entails, I must first look to myself to live out trustworthiness before I expect it from others. Remember the "Big 7"? I need to ask these attributes of myself before I ask them of others. I must go first.

In a world where we must aspire to trustworthiness, we must also accept that we will never live up to our own standards of it. This is why discipleship must entail not only the right aspirations but also the ability to ask forgiveness when we fail. We also must be people who forgive others when they fail.

> **A HUMBLE, FORGIVING HEART IS REQUIRED FOR RELATIONSHIPS WHEN EVERYONE IS BROKEN.**

A humble, forgiving heart is required for relationships when everyone is broken. Though we were the ones in the wrong, God made the first move to restore the relationship (Romans 5:6–8). He is the great reconciler, and now we are to be ministers of reconciliation. As those who look like Jesus, we make the first move.

Now some might ask, "What would happen if I did my part, and the other people don't? What if no matter what I do, others refuse to trust me? What if they are untrustworthy and controlling, and they won't work on their end of things?" Well, I am not saying there is never a time to go somewhere else, but it is never before we go first. We make the shift from skeptical to safe because Jesus went first and we are becoming more and more like him—not because we're following the other person's lead. Jesus went first, and some still didn't receive him. Like him, we do our part whether or not others do theirs. We don't wait for others to change before we move; we go first by doing what we can do.

THE LESSON WE LEARNED

So the better question is not whether I trust them but whether I am trustworthy to them. Do others trust me? Now, you might say, "Of course they trust me, or else they would tell me. Or I would just know." Maybe not, though. Most people aren't highly aware of how others perceive them. In fact, all the other people on your team probably think they are trustworthy too. And they often have their own reasons why they might not trust you.

Added to that, most people keep their perceptions to themselves. People are typically not courageous or honest in these areas. Besides, if there are ways in which you are unsafe, most people won't tell you because you are, well, unsafe. Maybe they won't share because they need a paycheck, and you are their boss. Maybe they don't want any office drama. Maybe they learned to live in an environment without trust, so they are used to it. Maybe they don't really want to have a relationship with you, so they don't see the need to invest in the relationship. However, if relationships in your home, church, or workplace are God's desire (and they are), then the trust issue must be dealt with. Not having trust isn't acceptable. This is one of the things discipleship is all about.

Fighting for a relationship with someone who is skeptical of you isn't easy and takes a lot of wrestling within yourself. It sure did (and does) for me. Not getting defensive, offended, disappointed, or ashamed can be extremely difficult. We will never get over this constant issue until we are in the new heaven and new earth. However, as people start to share their heart and the way they see things, something happens that changes the game. Mutual honesty can move you from becoming a group that just works together to one that loves and trusts one another. As you start to discover how other people see things, you start to deal with them differently. And they do the same with you. When people know each other's hearts and believe they are cared about, it's funny how so many of the things that used to offend you start to evaporate. You start to assume better over worse. When someone falls back into old patterns, you know why and are quickly able to help them change. When humility and understanding take over, things that once took forever can start to move at the pace of trust.

A SKEPTICAL WORLD

With increasing political polarization and institutional mistrust, it's easy to be skeptical of people. It's easy to stay guarded and suspicious, even when it comes to the people you work with. Yet if you're a leader, you'll want to remember that lack of trust is more than just hurtful to individual relationships;

it also hurts entire organizations. According to many surveys, people don't usually leave one job for another because of pay. They leave because there is a lack of relationship and trust. The cost of a loss of staff and a never-ending search for the next new person is immense.

But let's say you're a fairly suspicious person, and you just really have trouble trusting the people you work with. You wish you could get a feel for what they're really thinking. Okay, let's run with that. To really discover how people perceive you, here are some options:

1. You could become a fly on the wall of the coffee breakroom.
2. You could create a computer program to help you find out who the anonymous person on Facebook was that just trashed you.
3. You could learn to read people's minds or access the journal hidden under their bed.
4. You could make people mad enough over time that they blow up at you in a public way and let you know what they're thinking.

I hope you didn't read any of those and say, "You know, that might work!" It won't, and even if it could, paranoia isn't the way of Jesus.

Or how about this? You as a disciple maker could embrace a new understanding of what maturity looks like and decide that the maturity process starts with *you*. Most Christians were not shown healthy ways of dealing with conflict or differences in relationships. That's why the shifts we've been talking about are so important:

RelationShift 1: From Feed Me to Fellowship
RelationShift 2: From Friendliness to Love
RelationShift 3: From Recognition to Realness
RelationShift 4: From Skeptical to Safe

The focus of our attention needs to be on us becoming trustworthy and safe leaders who go first in trying to do what Jesus would do in every relationship situation. Here are some concrete ways we could do this:

1. Create clear expectations of what trustworthiness looks like and communicate them (for example, my "Big 7").
2. Seek to do your best to live and walk with integrity, and when you don't, ask for forgiveness even when people don't feel you failed.
3. Create a safe place to deal with conflict, present and imminent, by pre-emptively going first to make things safer for others to confront you as the leader.
4. Own your part in the conflict even if the other person doesn't own their part in it.
5. Go to someone first if you think they are angry at you, regardless of whether they come to you.
6. Praise people when they are honest with you even when you don't agree with them.

Starting with your own honesty and intentionality, you start to create a safe and trustworthy environment around yourself that allows others to be honest. As you model this, it can become the norm on your team. I'll mention that even if something like this doesn't happen, you're still following Jesus and making him proud. And for those who have chosen to be disciples of Jesus, you are becoming a model they can follow. This kind of leadership creates a trustworthy and safe place for you and the people you lead. You're beginning to establish a beachhead from which God can change a home, church, or work environment over time. This is the kind of environment where discipleship happens.

But couldn't all this relational focus start to blur important lines between leadership and personal relationships? How do we shift from skeptical to safe and yet retain the needed boundaries that keep people accountable in the realm of work? We'll delve into those important questions in the next chapter.

8

THE LEADERSHIP-RELATIONSHIP TENSION

How do we as leaders cultivate a safe approachability that doesn't go so far that it erodes needed accountability? How do we pursue genuine relationships while still maintaining leadership structure?

Many of the leaders and pastors/ministers our team works with have struggled to understand how it is possible to have an organizational structure and real relationships with the same people at the same time. I agree there is a tension and immaturity that can cause quite a problem if we don't deal with it.

We also have to remember that all of us can fall back into immaturity. I wish our hearts and minds were like a dial you turned to a specific place, and it never moved from there regardless of conditions, struggles, spiritual dryness, etc. I would love to come up with some sort of spiritual Loctite product that kept my spiritual maturity dials from moving. We also must acknowledge that though we love Jesus and have the Holy Spirit, there are more factors than just you and me. There is a spiritual enemy who deceives, corrupts, and divides. Even mature believers who have been friends for years often cannot recognize his ploys at the same time. Relationships can find themselves in unreconcilable seasons. Leadership dynamics make friendships harder. As a leader, I have to discern when I am supposed to lead, coach, and push, and when I am to be a friend who just listens and supports. Not every team stays together. Sometimes we have to fire people who have become friends. People can hurt us, and we can hurt them. Enough pain, and we can be tempted to give up on the whole relationship thing.

However, we have God's Word, which teaches and models both tears and truth instead of isolation and loneliness. With the Holy Spirit within and his Word to guide us, we can aim for and experience a healthy leadership-relationship balance. Just know it will be imperfect because we are all imperfect.

As we look at the early church, it seemed to be their aspiration to be characterized by structure and order, *as well as* relationship and mutual submission. In the book of Ephesians, Paul tells us that God appointed leaders in the church (Ephesians 4:11–13) and in the home (Ephesians 5:22ff). At the same time, we are called on to submit to one another out of reverence for Christ (Ephesians 5:21). Along with this, we are called on to love one another with sincere hearts and to lay down our rights for the good of one another. As an example, Timothy was told to command certain things but also to act as a brother (1 Timothy 4:11; 5:1). When to do what can be hard to figure out.

In a sense, the early church was like a car engine with many designed parts. As I mentioned in Chapter 4, these parts cannot function together without oil. Analogous to the parts of an engine, everybody in a church is equipped by the Holy Spirit with spiritual gifts so we can carry out the church's work (e.g., see Romans 12:3–8). Just as an engine needs oil, we need the Holy Spirit's presence and power to move us to love one another.

Thus, we work together in the context of fellowship rather than competing with and frustrating each other by demanding our own way and needing the spotlight. Without this "oil," friction will cause things to heat up and lead to an explosion.

People often want to lead because it fulfills the American dream to be on top. And, unfortunately, being on the bottom or anywhere near it often means you are treated as less than by your leaders and celebrated less by others in general. However, in the New Testament church, we see a growing Christlikeness that makes leaders more trustworthy. Because the apostles had been with Jesus, there had been changes in what leadership was all about. Leadership became more about protecting, serving, and loving others than about lording authority over others. The new disciples accepted the apostles' authority, as well as the value of those around them now that they were all in Christ.

As we follow Christ today, we should become more trustworthy and safer to be in relationship with, but this doesn't change the need for leadership and structure. As leaders spend time with Jesus today, they should become the kind of leaders that people can learn to trust.

STRUCTURE *AND* RELATIONSHIP

Over the years, I have heard many non-Christians, as well as immature Christians, say they don't want to be a part of an organized religion. Certainly, being in the wrong kind of organization with the wrong kind of people is often painful and overly exhausting and leads to few wins. At the same time, as I tell them, the same God who ordered the universe also orders the home and the church.

Many church leaders and pastors have made mistakes around the concept of organization within the church as well.

Some pastors will allow the church to be organized only to the extent that they themselves sit at the top of the organizational chart. Why?

- It might be because they have never been taught how a healthy organization can help accomplish the mission as well as help them thrive.
- It might be because they have been hurt by leaders, so they have decided against organization that puts them at risk from others.
- They may be limited in their administrative ability, so they don't know how to allow others onto a team that will expand the scope of the ministry they participate in.
- They may believe that too much organizing takes away from the Holy Spirit's power and leadership. It's true that people can get in the way of what the Spirit wants to do, but God's Holy Spirit has given us his holy Word—which describes God as a God of order (1 Corinthians 14:33).

And there could be other reasons as well.

Yet when we look at the early church as our model, we see that as the numbers flooded in, organization was required. As the church in Acts progressed and grew, order was needed because needs started to get overlooked, which affected people in negative ways. In Acts 6, when the Greek widows were going hungry, the apostles were humble enough to ask the people to help them choose seven Spirit-filled men to help gather supplies and distribute them to those in need. The early church ministered to not only their own but also to the needs of unbelievers. They enjoyed the favor of all the people (including non-believers). How could this be? Well, when you are relationally starving and you see people who are relationally full, it is hard not to want in. When you see people who are trustworthy enough to be real around, and you see people giving out help rather than judgment, it is hard to hate them.

It's not surprising that the church grew. If all the apostles did was teach and not raise up others or support and defend an environment where those practices were lived out, then the church's vision and aspirations would have been theoretical alone. It would have been a non-practical way of living that was unfulfilling and unconvincing.

Yet although there was structure in the early church, it wasn't a matter of climbing a hierarchy and enjoying power over others. Often, church leaders today think they must adopt the world's hierarchical leadership structure and model to be successful. Yet we see neither an obsession with control nor a spiral into chaos in the first church. There was clearly order and leadership, along with relationships. Rather than either/or, it was both.

At our church, we talk often about the bullseye of relational authority. I want you to take a look at the visual below and notice the person in the middle. Each and every person stands in their own circle like this, and the goal is that they will be growing in every direction.

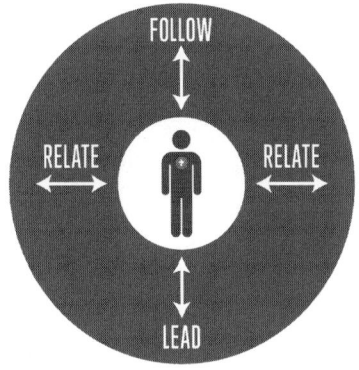

One of the most crucial ways you can cultivate healthy relationships in an organization is by being a safe person for others. As we look at each of these types of relationships, ask yourself if you are being a safe person in each.

BECOMING A SAFE PERSON FOR THOSE YOU FOLLOW

Let me give you an example of how it works in my life. At our church, I have the dual role of being both the senior pastor of Real Life Ministries and an elder on the eldership team.

As someone in the middle, I have an arrow pointing up. I am under the ultimate authority of Jesus, as this is his church. And I am also under the authority of the eldership as a whole. At our church, we believe that every person is under God-given human authority and needs accountability. No human is exempt from this, regardless of how high they may see themselves. As the British historian Lord Acton remarked, "Absolute power corrupts absolutely." I believe this is why God called for a plurality of elders rather than just one. As someone who answers to the eldership as God's delegated authority over our church, I must show humility and a willingness to serve in the way God leads our eldership to go as a whole.

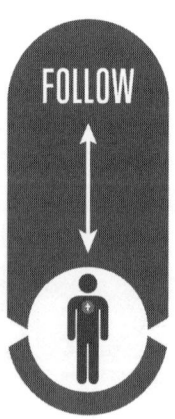

Those who are under authority need to understand that the leader needs relationships as much as they do. Being on top of the organizational chart carries with it far more weight than you would think. So many think they would like the benefits they perceive the leader gets, but they do not often think of the cost. Especially for someone in a spiritual leadership role, the devil will try to isolate the leader by telling them that no one understands. The enemy will try to convince the leader that the only reason people want to be their friend is to get an upper hand on the org chart.

The enemy will even use seemingly good intentions to isolate the leader. I know leaders who will do whatever they can to bless those who work for them. They will be the stopgap for any holes that arise. They will work long hours so others can get time off. They will spend so much time working for those they lead that they have no time for a relationship with anyone, including family. As an employee and a friend of this person over you, your role is to become trustworthy enough to be a help and support. Remember that, as disciples of Jesus, our responsibility is to do all we do unto the Lord (Colossians 3:23). Our role is more than just being an authority or under authority—it is also to build relational trust with people.

As a person under authority to others, I must be not only the kind of person who values and submits to authority but also the kind who allows for those above me to trust me as a friend. If someone is vulnerable with what they tell me and entrust to me, they must find me trustworthy.

UNSAFE FOLLOWER: ABSALOM

When I think of a person who was not a good follower yet loved by those below him, I think of Absalom, son of King David (2 Samuel 15–17). King David set aside a day each month to act as a judge. People would bring him their issues and disputes, and he would listen and rule on them. Absalom, bitterly jaded by having an unengaged father, concocted a scheme to make himself popular with the people so he could usurp the throne. As part of that scheme, he started meeting people at the palace gate before they could bring their issues to the king. He intentionally sought to make the kind of judgments—for the right kind of people—that would gain him influence.

Not everyone does this kind of usurping on purpose. For some, they do not like conflict, so rather than represent the team accurately, they will make themselves out to be the bearer of bad news—and the hero at the same time. They make it sound like they tried but could do nothing about the decision that was made.

Several years ago, I had a staff member who had been brought up from within our church to oversee many small groups and their leaders. I am going to tell you the story but change a few details to keep it anonymous. This man had a rough background, and through the years we poured so much into him. He became very influential and began to be perceived to be a great leader by those who followed him on the org chart. Monthly, we would gather as a team to determine the needs and direction of the groups as a whole. He would be a part of what would be decided and then go from there to lead the groups under his responsibility. Usually he agreed with the direction, and when he didn't, he would voice it. However, he never registered a strong disagreement that would have been considered serious.

At least from what the rest of the leaders could see.

As time went on, I started to hear rumblings from volunteer leaders under his leadership. In every case, they would share their frustration with our church and lead team, while their direct leader was always the hero in their eyes. When I asked what they would have us do differently, they said things like, "You should let [the leader in charge of our groups] lead." I brought in the staff member and told him what I was hearing. I explained, "You sit in meetings with us and help decide on the direction with us. You don't share any issues with us that your volunteer team may be having, and you're not sharing any disagreements with the direction we collectively decided on. So why do your people see you as the hero and the rest of us as the villains?"

As we talked, I realized that I had someone who was trustworthy in the eyes of those he led but not trustworthy to those who led him. He was creating an "us-vs-them" culture because of his lack of honesty. If we had known there had been a problem, we could have made different plans based on his feedback. But this leader wanted the love of his people so badly that whichever way they leaned, he joined them and blamed us. After many attempts to resolve this situation, the leader left the church. Several people rallied to him, but they never knew the full story.

Are you a safe person for the leaders you follow?

BECOMING A SAFE PERSON FOR THOSE YOU LEAD

I also have a down arrow, which in my case connects with our staff as a whole. The elders have given me the responsibility to oversee our staff. Because our staff is layered, I have an executive team underneath me, with everyone leading their own team, and so on. So I serve as an overseer on site in my role with the staff.

This kind of relationship is built over time as we set aside lines of authority and just talk about our real lives. For example, when we go hunting together, or golfing (I am terrible at it), or watch a game together, or play cards, we are just spiritual brothers, and there is no thought in those times of who is in charge. This development happens only when you value the other person and their maturity enough that you allow them to see the real you. Once they see the real you, they will notice that you are not perfect. Although that is nothing new to you, it may be to them, and they will have to be mature enough to handle it. You will have to be relationally mature enough to handle it too.

Difficulties do arise. It would be naïve to think they won't. But you must have a shared commitment to address the difficulties as they come up and set clear boundaries and rules for relationships (for me, these are my "Big 7"; see Chapter 7). Anytime you seek to have relationships, you inevitably will get hurt at points along the way, but rather than quitting, you go back to the person and do what love requires. 1 Corinthians 13 tells us that love keeps no record of wrongs, and it always perseveres. Love is honest and tells the truth rather than allowing pride in and hiding being your position. I am not saying that you must cultivate deep relationships with everyone, but for a relational/family environment to exist, everyone needs a relationship with someone (in fact, more than someone—with a group). A church is supposed to be a safe place to work, but it goes beyond that; it needs to be full of safe people who truly become family. We are part of the family of God, and this moves us past the realm of friendly-but-shallow relationships.

I am so blessed to have many people on my team who can speak truth into my life on many issues as much as or more than I speak into their lives. I may be the leader of the staff organizationally, but many of them have been married longer, or been a Christian longer, or have had more experience with a number of things than I have. And no matter what I may know or what skills I may have, I am still capable of having a rotten attitude or becoming proud. As my brothers or sisters, they have an obligation to lovingly tell me when I am not acting in a mature way. If I must know the most about everything and can't stomach ever being wrong, then I have a pride problem, and I desperately need these relationships.

To use a football analogy, the head coach wants to hire someone who knows more about defense than he does, so he hires the best defensive coordinator. The best coaches I know lead in such a way that they want the best people on the team giving the best guidance in their particular area. They also want the greatest *people* too because it's the great relationships and fun that get them through the intense ups and downs of the season. Doing life (not just work) with the people you lead requires you to walk a sometimes-difficult balance, but it's worth it. Relationship is important for your well-being and theirs.

RECOGNIZING TEMPTATIONS

When we're the leader, it's easy to get lazy about Jesus' authority over us and assume that we're in charge. We must remember that following Jesus supersedes organizational structure. Whether I am over you or under you or side-by-side with you, we are brothers and sisters in Christ, called to work together for the Lord's glory. Just because I am the boss does not give me the right to set aside biblical behavior. No matter where you are on the organizational chart, there is a process for dealing with sin that must be followed. The boss has no exemption from the Matthew 18 disciplinary restoration process.

So in my down arrow, I need to lead like Jesus leads. That means I don't simply do whatever my down line wants. Jesus led his disciples where his *Father* wanted him to lead them, and at times his disciples didn't necessarily like the direction he led. Yet it was always for their good. As a leader, Jesus cared for his disciples and was trustworthy in every respect. Even when his disciples behaved immaturely, he remained trustworthy.

Over the years, I have worked with people who did a good job of following their boss yet did a poor job of leading those assigned to them. So their up arrow was good, but their down and side-to-side arrows were not. I once had a leader underneath me that took care of so many of the details I often missed. We all have holes in our game, and I needed someone to fill them for me. Although this person was helpful to me, I found out, after too long, that he was being harmful to the team down the line.

Once I figured this out, an analogy came to me that made total sense. Have you ever seen one of those little dogs that is so loving to their master but will bite anyone else that comes near them? This was what this situation was like for me. Often, the owner of the dog doesn't know about the situation until someone comes to visit. Then, suddenly, there is growling and barking that they wouldn't have believed could come out of their little loving friend.

Sometimes a leader will be devoted to one person who will be so important to their own job that it makes sense to keep them on, no matter the cost to the whole team. In my case, people knew I needed the kind of help this person was giving me, and they knew I really loved the guy. So they didn't say anything—until one day when they were bit one too many times. At first I thought it was the "victim's" fault. However, the truth started to come out more and more, and that's when I realized I had a real problem. Some people down the line thought I was aware of what was happening and was basically condoning it. They had started to judge my heart and others' because the problem was never addressed. So after many attempts at trying to help this well-intentioned but clueless leader, I knew I could not have a leader in a position that affected our culture in this way.

Often, the trouble is in the leader seeing the task as more important than the people. So to speed things up, perhaps they just send an abrupt email or simply text someone information instead of talking things through relationally. (I admit that at times that I can fall into this too—most busy people do.) They inform people about the "what" and not the "why." The heart behind the decision ends up lost in translation, and people get hurt. So, if you want to have a relational culture, you must discern rightly about what topics need to be talked through and what can be dealt with via email. You need to move more slowly so that trust is preserved. Relationships matter more than getting tasks done quickly, so we must move at a speed that preserves trust.

> **WE MUST MOVE AT A SPEED THAT PRESERVES TRUST.**

Sometimes people who are not relational can tend to appear authoritarian in their leadership style. They do what they are told because their leader is "the boss." And then they expect those they lead to do the same. It's true that we should have a humble spirit with our leaders, but that humility should extend both ways. A humble leader seeks to listen well and adjust where they are able while still leading the right direction.

REMEMBERING WHAT'S IMPORTANT

As I mentioned earlier, some leaders have been taught that you cannot be in a leadership role over someone and it be an honest Christian relationship at the same time. I cannot tell you how strongly I disagree with this, though I have had many experiences that would make it easy to believe that. It may be easier to be in one or the other, but as believers we are not called to do the easy thing. Safe relationships are worth the effort.

I am blessed to have some of my best friends be under my authority on the org chart. But the org chart does not dictate how we relate to each other normally. In some settings, I am the boss, but I am called to be a relationally trustworthy boss who creates a safe place to be real. And at the end of those occasions when I have a job-related authority responsibility, I am still just a regular guy whose core identity doesn't come with an authority label on my forehead. We are just friends doing life together. For sure, there have been times when I had to make a leadership decision that affected one of my friends, and our commitment to work through this together makes it possible.

For instance, I may have had to move them from one position to another, or even remove them from a staff position altogether, but because of our deep relationship, we were able to make it through. It takes incredible maturity on their part to be committed enough to the Lord and to our relationship to work it through. But our maturity is tested and proven when we deal with these kinds of issues.

BECOMING A SAFE PERSON FOR YOUR PEERS

I also have arrows that go side-to-side. This represents the peer-to-peer relationships I have with others. In this area, I have relationships that have no official lines of authority at all other than the mutual submission we give to one another (Ephesians 5:21). For me, this includes the fellow elders I am in relationship with. The elders at the church I serve are my peers, but some are also my closest friends, and the topic of authority plays no part when we're spending time relationally.

As my peers, they have the responsibility to speak truth to me as a friend and co-laborer. If I listen only to those who have organizational authority over me, then I am missing the mutual Christian submission to one another described in the New Testament. As colleagues and friends, we may share the same position on an org chart, but our alignment, or lack thereof, can affect the morale or success of the total effort. As both friends and peers, we allow each other to speak truth to one another, much like David and Jonathan did in the Old Testament story of their friendship.

Honestly, it can be easier to have an authentic relationship with someone who is not in your up or down line. But peer-to-peer relationships can still be sabotaged by a lack of communication or by jealousy. For example, when someone on the org chart in another area gets resources you didn't or is celebrated more than your part of the team, it can spark a spirit of competition or bitterness. This can lead to merely surface relationships and working in silos. Our responsibility is to constantly allow the Holy Spirit to help us see where our flesh, their flesh, and the devil are working against real relationship and then fight against these forces (or at least stop it on our side of the equation). We must be vigilant and diligent to work through issues as they come up. The devil plays on our emotions and our egos. It takes mature people to see what he is doing and turn back his efforts.

THE SILO MAN

Several years ago, I had a leader who did a great job of being under relational authority. I trusted him, and he trusted me. He also was beloved by those he led. However, when it came to his relationship with his peers on staff, there was constant tension. As team members, we may have differing job responsibilities, but we must remember there is a shared overall goal we must be aligned with and pursue. Instead of working together relationally to be a people who loved one another well, this man had little use for the people on the other teams.

When there were projects that differed and teams should have been able to work together, he wasn't interested unless he had positional authority over others from the other teams involved. This led to a lack of unity and desired results, and, more importantly to me, it led to anything but a relational environment where he was involved—that is, anywhere he was involved outside of his own designated responsibilities. He led in such a way that silos developed, and eventually he had to leave. It was such a sad day for me. I just couldn't understand why he would not do the same kinds of things with others that he was willing to do on his own team.

Siloing ourselves is detrimental to the team, and whatever is detrimental to the Lord's team impacts his mission for us. Developing mature disciples who understand relationships—what it takes to create them and how to protect them—must be the goal of the whole team. So often we just put our head down and focus on tasks because they are easier, but God calls us to focus on relationships. The scriptural directions for trustworthiness determine the trustworthiness of a peer.

DISCOVERING YOUR BLIND SPOTS

In each of the negative cases I have relayed, there was a blind spot in the leaders' lives. Other than the Absalom story I shared, I don't think any of the other leaders intended to be divisive or to frustrate people. In each case, these people loved Jesus and wanted to do a good job. However, they could not see their blind spot and were unwilling or unable to accept that it was there and make the change.

If we are to have a relational environment, we need the humility to know that wherever we go we may be a part of the problem. We are all broken, and many times we don't even know in what ways. So first, we have to accept that fact. Second, we must allow God to use others to help us see where we are missing the mark. This means seeking honest feedback about our blind spots. The best leaders never stop learning. Every great athlete has a coach. Some athletes, however, have holes in their game but do not want to be coached. Affirmed, yes; coached, no. We must seek to become aware of our strengths and our weaknesses, and the only way that happens is if we not only accept that we have both but that we also have others who can help us to determine what both really are.

THE BEST LEADERS NEVER STOP LEARNING.

When it comes to developing a relational environment, we need to get honest feedback about where we fit in these relationships. Am I a safe person for the people leading me? Am I a safe person for the people I lead? Am I a safe person for my peers? The only way you will know for sure is if you get honest feedback. The only way I know to become accurate in my awareness is to allow others from the outside to help me discover this.

To delve deeper into discovering your own blind spots, I encourage you to work through Appendix B: American Idol Exercise.

ARE YOU TRUSTWORTHY?

So we see that in all three kinds of relationships (up, down, and side-to-side) we are called to be trustworthy and safe to allow for honesty, accountability, and support. Recall my "Big 7" in Chapter 7 on the seven attributes I use to judge my own trustworthiness and others' trustworthiness as well.

In these areas of our lives, we must live out a blending of leadership and relational trustworthiness. We may not have leadership responsibilities in some of the roles we are in, but as disciples of Jesus we are definitely influencers who change the environment wherever we are. We abide in Christ and seek to understand his will, and then we go first to live that out in our human relationships.

Before we move into the fifth RelationShift, pray and ask yourself if you are trustworthy. In which environments (up, down, side-to-side) do you need to discover your blind spots? What do you need to do to become more of a safe follower, leader, and peer? When (not if) you discover areas you need to change, how do you do that? The only one who scores perfect in every environment is Jesus.

You've come across some helpful ideas in these chapters. It's easy to hear them, get inspired, but then do nothing. To build the kinds of relationships that cultivate discipleship we must make the final shift—from idea to implementation. The following chapters wrestle very specifically with the "how."

AN AUTHORITY OF TRUSTWORTHINESS EXERCISE

As a team, review the seven elements of trustworthiness that follow (what I call my "Big 7"). Do you think this is a good list in your context? What would you add or remove? As a team, take some time to modify this list together or create an agreed-upon new list that will guide your relationships with each other:

1. Courage

- You speak the truth in love even when it is hard.
- You tell me what I need to hear rather than I want to hear.

2. Honesty

- You keep your word.
- You tell me the truth about yourself.
- You don't lie.

3. Humility

- You are coachable.
- You can admit to being wrong, and you can ask for forgiveness.

4. Loyalty

- You don't gossip.
- You don't run for cover when it gets hard to be a friend.
- You defend me to others even if it costs you to do so.
- You give me the benefit of the doubt when you hear things about me you don't like and will come to me personally to address it.

5. Wisdom

- Scripture guides your perspective and actions.
- As someone who desires wisdom, you consider others' perspective when you deal with things they are responsible for or are connected to.

6. Reconciliation

- You point me and others to God's heart when conflict arises.
- Your goal is to put out fires rather than pour gas on them.
- You fight for the restoration of relationship.

7. Forgiveness

- Our relationship will not be easy to break.
- Even when we fail, we know we will work it out.

SHIFT

5

From Idea to Implementation

9

RELATIONAL SYSTEMS

I t's really easy to pick up a book like this, say, "Wow, those are helpful ideas," and then file it away under the category of good ideas you'd like to revisit if you ever get the time. As a busy church leader, you're used to having to say no to good, even great, ideas. There's a sermon to write by the end of the week, after all.

In the next couple chapters, I want to show you how this shift to a relational focus as the context for discipleship is so much more than just a good idea theoretically. It really can become a game changer in your church as you implement relational systems churchwide. You really can do this. And it really is worth it.

As you are probably aware by now, I believe that every church leader is a disciple maker along with every other disciple of Jesus. Not everyone has the call to leadership within the church, but to those who do, we are given the task to help organize the church in such a way that every Christian has the opportunity to live the disciple's life in practice. I'd like to share with you how our church has chosen to develop a reproducible model of disciple making and leadership development that's based on relationship more than information.

When a church leader takes the following five steps, they help their church transition from information-based systems to relationship-based systems. The following five steps show how you can implement the ideas in this book churchwide.

1. Model what you want the church to do.

As I write this chapter, our Real Life Ministries staff sits at well over a hundred people. Almost every one of those staff members came from right here in the northern Idaho area. So how did they get on staff? They joined us not merely because they knew the Bible well or because they had leadership capabilities but also because they became disciples in relationships. This may have happened somewhere else, or they may have learned it here, but without it they would not be on our team. They then learned to make that kind of disciple as well. They learned to develop and care for disciple makers before we brought them on staff.

In other words, they must prove they were gifted as coaches before they graduate to that role. You might think that now that they lead disciple making *systems*, these staff members have graduated from actual disciple making. But that would be a faulty assumption.

At Real Life, people not only get on staff by proving they are a disciple maker; they stay on staff by being a disciple maker. We have a two-tiered work plan here. We have a *Ministry Plan* that mirrors the same forty-hour work week every other believer has in their regular job (actually, more hours in many staff jobs). We then have a *Personal Ministry Plan* (roughly ten hours) that everyone on staff, including our pastors, follows as well. I'll go into more detail on those two plans in Chapter 11.

In that ten-hour Personal Ministry Plan, our staff are in small groups doing relational discipleship just as we ask every believer with regular jobs to do. The people in our church have a regular job, where they work forty hours a week and balance their family as well. We ask our people to be in church services, be in a life group, and if capable, to lead a group too. If we ask this of them, why would we allow our staff to do any less? What we ask others to do, we do too.

Earlier, I mentioned how Matthew 23:4 had impacted me: "They tie up heavy, cumbersome loads and put them on other people's shoulders, but they themselves are not willing to lift a finger to move them." We are determined not to put burdens on our people that we don't carry ourselves. Not only does this standard keep our staff connected to the actual work of a disciple maker, it also keeps them connected relationally with those they disciple. Remember, Jesus' methods for disciple making not only work best but they also produce the relational connectedness we all need in our lives so that we can live out the ministry he has given us. God's version of relationships provides the spiritual energy needed for ministry.

2. Create a system of ministry that enables people to be relationally discipled within your church.

Some pastors can try so hard to disciple everyone that they don't end up discipling anyone to maturity, and they also don't experience the real relationships they themselves need. A pastor or leader cannot disciple everyone. Their role is making disciples who can make disciples. At Real Life, our system of life groups is developed in such a way that our people can experience relational discipleship for themselves.

The discipleship system you create needs to provide the following (although this is not a comprehensive list):

A. Consistent alignment around shared language, goals, and methods
B. Leadership oversight with training/coaching
C. Discipline and protection where needed
D. Pastoral care for the leaders
E. Oversight of curriculum to protect right doctrine

3. Make sure they keep the main thing the main thing (relational discipleship).

It's natural to see discipleship in the church as yet another program alongside the others. *(Isn't that what the discipleship minister is supposed to be doing?)* As such, discipleship can be seen as a competitor with other church functions. This is why it's crucial to align all ministries according to the part they play in keeping the main thing the main thing. As an example, the point of assigning leaders to oversee the distribution of food in the early church (Acts 6:1–7) was not to add another program but to delegate the responsibility to others so that the apostles could keep the main thing the main thing. "We will turn this responsibility over to them and will give our attention to prayer and the ministry of the word" (Acts 6:3b–4). The result: "So the word of God spread. The number of disciples in Jerusalem increased rapidly" (Acts 6:7a).

At Real Life, we have weekend services, mid-size group meetings, house group meetings, and one-on-one meetings. We have ministries for the poor, for recovering addicts, for people interested in sports, and so on. However, none of these replace relational discipleship. In fact, they are all intentionally structured to feed into relational discipleship. Every door leads to relational discipleship. Again, we've structured each of these ministries to be in conjunction with relational discipleship. However, if it ever comes to the place where a person only has time for one thing, I want it to be relational discipleship.

EVERY DOOR LEADS TO RELATIONAL DISCIPLESHIP.

4. Protect the church from those who divide or distract from relational discipleship.

Most every pastor and leadership team want their church to grow. Sometimes they make the mistake of trying to compete with Hollywood to do it. We cannot and should not try to compete with the entertainment industry. In the first book I wrote (*Church Is a Team Sport*), I shared that even the greatest movie can get boring after watching it a few times. If you try to compete with Hollywood, not only will you lose because you don't have their money, but you will also have to keep changing all the time or people will get bored. Our mission is to grow people up, not give the immature what they want.

Yet you will also have people who will come with all kinds of ideas about how to grow people up into maturity—ideas that can distract from relational discipleship. Perhaps they think you need to teach more about a particular topic. Perhaps they want you to preach according to a particular methodology. Perhaps they want more classroom-type environments. Whatever the case, they have a particular bent or passion, and they want you to join with them in it. Yes, God brings people to our churches to help us accomplish his mission in our area. And sometimes we should include them in what we can do together. Yet, as I will continue to say, our mission is to make mature disciples who make disciples. *That's* the mission. When we keep this focus and don't drift, we end up launching a spiritually trained and relationally supported army into everywhere they work, live, and play.

To do this, we must protect the mission God has given us. Our values, language, and methods protect us from getting off course. For every exciting idea you decide to run with, you make it impossible to do something else. That's called "opportunity cost." For this reason, be very careful whom you choose to celebrate and to whom you choose to give influence when you are leading. Remember, your people only have so much time. If you get them involved in too many things, you lead them toward a "rock skipping," surface-level relational life within your church (see Chapter 5). Without the time it takes to cultivate deep and real relationships, people will fall back on the shallow ones that don't sustain their faith for the long haul.

5. Decide on an entry point that gets your team on the same page.

At Real Life, people who want to join the church (to be "part of the team") attend a membership class. In this class, we typically have people from at least fourteen different denominations/forms of Christianity, as well as people from non-Christian backgrounds. Because we want to protect our people from influences that divide us, this class explains what we believe before people commit. We want them to know what we believe about salvation, and if they are not yet believers, we want to present the gospel to them.

If they are believers, we want to teach them what we consider to be essential issues versus nonessential issues so they can decide if they agree with us right out of the gate. Our leaders explain where the church came from, where we are going, what we believe, what we expect, and what they can expect from us so that they can make an informed decision to continue or not. If a person decides to be on our team, we then help them find a place to connect beyond our large group gatherings where they can connect in real relationships and learn to serve God and others.

Remember that every door leads to relational discipleship where our introductory language gains a practical life that can be modeled and followed.

THE CENTRALITY OF A GROUP

At Real Life, all roads lead to getting people into small groups (what we call life groups) because in our context, that's where relational discipleship happens best. In other contexts, churches experience relational discipleship best in even smaller groups (e.g., gender-specific groups of three to four people, what my friend and Discipleship.org leader Bobby Harrington calls "transformation groups").

I have personally been in a weekly mixed-gender life group for over thirty years. I cannot tell you how many times we have multiplied our group. During the summer, my wife and I take a break from having a mixed-gender weekly meeting in the home, and I meet with my men's group. We do things like dinners, camping, coffee, etc. During that time, I hope to see the guys with their families, and they get to see me with mine in regular real-world settings. I get to see who they are without their church and group face on so that I can know who they really are behind the scenes.

Relational discipleship can be fun, and just enjoying our-selves with no agenda is a huge part of relationship and of liv-ing the authentic life of a disciple. Then, in the fall, we start up our regular group times again.

GROUP EXPECTATIONS

When we start our regular group times, we always start with setting the stage for what this group is going to look like. I share that I am not just about connection in small groups but about *relational discipleship*. Many have been in a small group before, but that doesn't always result in more mature believers. I also share that the goal is that everyone here will be become mature in Christ and be able to make disciples in every part of their lives.

Not everyone is a future group leader, but some are, and I will be looking for an apprentice if I haven't already identified one. I share with them that many people out there need what we have in Christ. I often remind them that they all know and love someone who is lost, and they have probably been praying for them. If this group is just a closed clique that meets our own needs, then we have forgotten that discipleship is like a plane with two wings. Wing one is a family in relationship, matur-ing in our faith. Wing two is a body with a mission to reach lost people.

If we focus only on the relational wing, then we'll fly in a circle and crash. If we focus only on the mission side, we'll cir-cle and crash. We must have both to function as God intended.

I also try to help them understand my role as the group leader. I am not going to try to be the center of relationship for this group. My wife and I are going to invest as much as we can, but I am going to ask them over and over again to reach out to others in the group. Different people have different life seasons they are in. I'm trying to connect people who are in similar seasons. Also, it's really important that the older men invest in the younger men and the older women invest in the younger women. And whenever someone has an issue come up, we all can each offer help with our own unique contributions.

I then make the point that we are going to study the Scriptures together, but that everything we study will be directed at relationship with God and with one another. I share with them concepts found in this book about what relationships look like and the benefits for them. I also share that having a theoretical relationship with each other will be tempting and easier than actual, practical relationships. I share that the time you put in and the commitment to certain practices will determine what you get out. As you might guess, I don't talk through these things only the first time we meet; I beat this drum over and over in a variety of ways. For additional "relational rules" we go through in our life groups, check out Appendix C: Expectations and Assumptions for Small Groups.

These relational systems will help your church shift from idea to implementation. But—and I can't emphasize this enough—you cannot just ask other people to do this. This book describes shifts that even the most charismatic, visioneering leader cannot implement unless they themselves are committed in their core.

So how committed to church relationships are you? You'll find out when you face what tests every church to the core and burns some down: *conflict*.

10

NOT SO BAD

The movie *Rocky III* takes place after Rocky Balboa has become the heavyweight boxing champion by defeating Apollo Creed in *Rocky II*.[10] With Rocky's newfound celebrity, stardom begins to fill him up to where he's no longer got the hunger needed to stay on top. He gets knocked out in the first round by the first real contender in months, Clubber Lang, played by a pugnacious Mr. T. As Rocky's trainer Mick explains, "The worst thing happened to you that could happen to any fighter. You got civilized."

The loss to Clubber Lang deflates him. Even as Rocky trains to fight him and take back the title, he's afraid and wants to back out. He explains to his wife, "I don't wanna lose what I got. At first, I didn't care about what happened. I'd go in the ring, get busted up. I didn't care! For the first time in my life, I'm afraid."

As happens in the *Rocky* movies, Rocky gets inspired, gets his "eye of the tiger" back, does a training montage to '80s rock music to prepare for the fight, and then the stage is set for the central fight of the movie. Now it's Clubber Lang who's gotten comfortable at the top, while Rocky's hunger has brought the old Rocky back. He's trained harder than Lang, and while

Lang's punches pack thunder, Rocky's stamina is clearly out-lasting Lang's. Even as Lang lands punch after punch, the exertion is wearing out Lang, to the point where Rocky begins taunting him: "You ain't so bad! Ain't so bad!"

In church leadership, it's easy to get domesticated and lose our hunger to make disciples and push back the darkness. It's easier to keep what we already have than to move the needle into what could be. It's easier to maintain than to push ahead.

When we find ourselves "civilized" in this way, we get scared of what we think will mess everything up: conflict. Con-flict within the church feels like it could unravel our success, and it becomes natural not to want anything to do with it. Like a self-fulfilling prophecy, conflict grows in the shadow of our passivity into something that really can mess things up.

Yet when we get hungry to make disciples in relationship, conflict becomes inevitable. It's just part of the process. So when we lean into the conflict, instead of shying away from it, we find out that conflict actually ain't so bad. By God's grace and through his wisdom, we can outlast the conflict and even use it for kingdom advancement.

CONFLICT MEANS COACHING OPPORTUNITIES

As church leaders, we're not directors trying to direct the best show for spectators; rather, we're coaches trying to coach our team into maturity. If we were mainly putting on a show, we would fear imperfect performances and not hand opportunities to anybody who didn't nail their lines perfect-ly. Yet we're coaches, and as such we need to be unafraid of coaching opportunities.

It's helpful to be reminded of our heritage. Going back to the beginning, we see that Jesus chose ordinary, unschooled men to be his disciples. He did this to show us that he is the one who gets the glory and that he can change the world with regular people. He didn't just call the talented or wise. The Gospels depict one extraordinary Messiah coaching a bunch of disciples who weren't just ordinary; they were *extra* ordinary. Intellectually, relationally, and spiritually, their report cards show C after C, with a few random As and Fs sprinkled in. The result was a group that went on to change history.

The roadway to maturity is filled with mistakes. You cannot get good at the game by sitting on the bench. You have to play. You will make mistakes, and you will need coaching. A coach doesn't see a player's mistake as a doorway to the bench but rather a doorway to improvement if the player is willing to learn. A coaching mindset gives people the space to play and get coached along the way. Through trial and error, our people get better at leading worship, or speaking, or leading a small group, and so on.

Yet so many churches don't let a person play until they get good at playing. How does that make any sense? Letting people play and coaching them through trial and error makes sense in sports, as well as in any skill you learn. When you think about it, it should make sense when it comes to church as well.

Even people who embrace the idea of coaching when it comes to church work can miss it when we are speaking about relationships. People in our culture often don't know what relationships should look like. Many Christians have sat in our auditoriums but have never actually been coached in real time on relationships. Why would they naturally be very good at it then, when you think about all the factors lined up against them?

When we shift to seeing relationships through the lens of coaching a team, not directing a performance, it becomes clear that conflict isn't something to be afraid of. Rather, when it comes to relationships, leaning into conflict instead of shying away from it gives us some of our best coaching opportunities.

YOU DON'T MAKE PEACE BY IGNORING CONFLICT

One of the most prominent themes of the Bible is forgiveness. God forgives us and expects us to forgive others. Yet forgiveness can take some intentionality. When it comes to significant conflict, the path to forgiveness and reconciliation isn't a matter of bypassing the conflict and pretending that everything is already fine. The more serious the conflict, the more likely it will require us to do more than just wave the hand and say, "Oh, I forgive you."

Unfortunately, we are often passive and disengaged in the realm of broken relationships. Jesus calls us to be peacemakers (Matthew 5:9). He is the Prince of Peace (Isaiah 9:6), and we are being conformed into his likeness (Romans 8:29). Jesus tells us that we are to initiate reconciliation wherever we are able and led to do so. For those who think they can have a good relationship with him but do nothing about resolving conflict with others, these words of Jesus should shake us awake:

> Therefore, if you are offering your gift at the altar and there remember that your brother or sister has something against you, leave your gift there in front of the altar. First go and be reconciled to them; then come and offer your gift. (Matthew 5:23–24)

In our times, this would mean that we seek reconciliation as best we can with another believer. If we are trying to please the Lord, we must take responsibility for our part of any broken relationship. We are called on to fight for the relationship, to go to the offended person and make it right. Of course there is no guarantee that the other will accept our attempt to make things right. Paul's caveats are instructive: *"If it is possible, as far as it depends on you, live at peace with everyone"* (Romans 12:18).

This means that we are to do all we can from our side of the problem to make things right. If we have done that, then we are right with the Lord. Yet, so often, we don't want to deal with conflict, so we just bury our heads in the sand and hope the problem goes away. The devil is a divider, and he will feed this division and make it grow. As Ephesians 6:12 reminds us, we do not wrestle against flesh and blood but against spiritual forces in the heavenly realms.

Every sports team coach knows that if the team is fighting in the locker room or in the huddle, they'll get owned on the line of scrimmage. It doesn't matter how much talent you have on your team. If a house is divided, it cannot stand, as Jesus told us in Mark 3:25. In the same way, the enemy defeats us when we turn our weapons inward at one another. Paul, writing to the Corinthian church, said it this way:

> The very fact that you have lawsuits among you means you have been completely defeated already. Why not rather be wronged? Why not rather be cheated? (1 Corinthians 6:7)

When there's significant conflict, peace via passivity isn't real peace. Peacemakers lean in and work for reconciliation.

IGNORING A LIT FUSE

The other day, I met with another church leadership team that was in conflict. They made it clear that they did not trust each other, and after a continued time of disagreement, they said, "Let's just move on. We are never going to see eye to eye. It would be better just to figure out how to move forward."

The pastor said, "Our mission is to reach the world, and this conflict is taking too much time and distracting from it." One of the other elders offered, "Let's figure out how to grow the church so we can hire more pastors to take the pressure off of the staff we have."

One of the other leaders then asked me, "Jim, why do you think we have flatlined and even declined? Can you help us come up with a strategy to reach our city?"

My response was not what they wanted to hear. I replied, "Based on what you guys just did, you have doomed yourself to decline. Before you can do anything to reach people, you must *be* a certain kind of people. Being is always first, then doing."

I went on to share that God is the one who adds to the number daily those who are being saved (Acts 2:42–47). I asked them, "Why would God add to your number when you have a bomb with a lit fuse that's going destroy those who are already in the church?"

Unresolved conflict and resentment cannot be overlooked because the devil uses them to destroy the Lord's work. I continued, "It is the same kind of thing an immature couple says when they are having trouble in their marriage. Rather than deal with their issues, they convince themselves that having another baby or buying a new house will somehow resolve their conflict. Nope! More kids mean more sleepless nights and stress, same with getting another house." My point was that until they actually resolved the issues and began loving each other well, I didn't think the Lord was going to help them reach more people. Strategy is important, but it never supersedes relationships.

As believers we are called on to mature to the point that any unresolved conflict is first on our priority list to deal with. Maturity means dealing with conflict rather than running away from it or acting like it doesn't exist.

The following are six principles for resolving conflict. We remind our staff and church of them often.

1. Deal with issues as they come up honestly and quickly.

Ephesians 4:25–27 says, "Therefore each of you must put off falsehood and speak truthfully to your neighbor, for we are all members of one body. 'In your anger do not sin': Do not let the sun go down while you are still angry, and do not give the devil a foothold."

As disciples of Jesus, we tell each other the truth rather than avoid the real issues. We do it quickly because the devil sees division in the same way a shark sees blood in the water. He smells it and comes looking for a meal. The point of this passage isn't that we must never go to bed until the issue is resolved but rather that we don't give conflict time to create bitterness in our hearts. Time allows the enemy to fill in the gaps with deception where there is a lack of clarity. The enemy loves to plant negative thoughts in our heads when we're wondering why someone acted a certain way or didn't respond to our attempts at all.

Before meeting together to talk things over, here are some helpful steps to think through:

- *P – Pray.* Praying before tough conversations keeps God and his will center stage (instead of your own grievances and desired outcomes). Praying helps you get in the right attitude and can help cool you down. Most importantly, we pray to ask God for his help because these sorts of situations are bigger than we can fix with our own power.
- *A – Admit.* If there's anything you could have handled better, it's good to lead the conversation with admitting it. Humility encourages humility. Hard truth may still be coming, but if you wish you had done anything better (and if you try, usually you can think of something), it's better to be upfront with this.
- *L – Listen.* It's easy to talk more than listen, but being too quick to talk and dominate the conversation will keep walls of hostility intact. As James 1:19b says, "Everyone should be quick to listen, slow to speak and slow to become angry."
- *S – Specify.* Specify what the actual problem is. The problem isn't the person. Rather, if you can specify what the actual problem is, then *together* you can confront the actual problem. This way you're on the same team trying to tackle the issue together. Avoid generalized language such as "you always" or "you never."

2. Deal with the issue privately before you bring someone else into the equation (exceptions may exist when dealing with someone of the opposite sex).

Matthew 18:15–17 says:

> If your brother or sister sins, go and point out their fault, just between the two of you. If they listen to you, you have won them over. But if they will not listen, take one or two others along, so that "every matter may be established by the testimony of two or three witnesses." If they still refuse to listen, tell it to the church; and if they refuse to listen even to the church, treat them as you would a pagan or a tax collector.

I truly believe that dealing with an offense starts with quickly and privately going to the person you are struggling with. I would add the truth that we often misunderstand each other, so rather than assuming the worst and accusing, I want to come in curious. Rather than coming to conclusions myself, I want to ask questions and listen. Remember, the devil wants us to come to quick decisions based on assumptions that do not give the benefit of the doubt. We have to cut him off at the pass.

To go and talk to another person about the problem, rather than first talking to the person with whom you have conflict, quickly turns into gossip. If you need wise counsel first, make sure you go to a person who is godly and is a peacemaker rather than someone who pours gasoline on the fire. If you do talk with someone else about the situation, don't identify who you're talking about. You do not want to damage a person's reputation with someone else.

3. Work on not becoming defensive. Celebrate the courage it took to be honest.

How we respond when someone talks to us about a problem will often determine whether they ever do it again. Handling it poorly without integrity can quickly earn you a reputation that says you are more interested in being right than in a relationship. Rarely are we all in the right, so we often have to own our part of the problem. If we were misunderstood, we may have to ask forgiveness for how we said it and then communicate what we were trying to say. This in particular has been a constant struggle for me in my leadership journey. I often forget that we are not battling over just an idea; often, people are attached to their idea and are hurt by what they deem personal to them.

Even if you disagree with what the other person says or thinks, thank them for having the honor and courage to deal with conflict in a courageous way. Resolving an issue may not be possible if listening to another person requires agreeing with them. However, you can share your heart with them so they understand the reason behind the decision and that you value them personally, even if you disagree with their opinion on something.

Offer to pray about it and even get wise counsel from others to double-check on the particular situation. Make it clear that by getting wise counsel, you are not using that as a euphemism for gossiping to gain support. Rather you're wanting to see if the idea they present has more merit than you think it does. I have found that, many times, people want you to agree, and you may not be able to. However, if you listen and show you care, they often at least feel heard. This allows the issue to become an agree-to-disagree situation, rather than a time to separate for good. By handling things this way, you are also modeling what disagreement looks like on your team so that those you are leading can do with others what you are modeling.

4. After there is a confrontation, go back later to check on how the other is doing.

Because conflict resolution is often not merely a one-time conversation, it takes relational tenacity to get through to resolution. Most people do not process quickly enough in the heat of the moment to say all they wanted to say. They also might get caught by something you said and not hear the rest. When the disagreement is over, the processing time begins. This is often when the enemy gets involved and starts to fill in the gaps. He tries to get you to focus on one thing the other person said rather than all that they said or the spirit in which they tried to say it.

> IT TAKES RELATIONAL TENACITY TO GET THROUGH TO RESOLUTION.

This is why it is so important to take this next step. You might think it's over and all is well, but don't make that mistake. Check in and ask them how they are doing after processing. You might ask, "Is there more we need to do to get through this together?"

Remember that many people take home the interaction to process with another person (e.g., their spouse). If they are processing with someone who wasn't there or is biased toward the person who is sharing, then this often doesn't lead to proper processing that leads to reconciliation. Rather it can pour gasoline on a small fire to cause it to blaze out of control. It can be difficult to seek out wise, impartial counsel in these kinds of supercharged situations and not spread hostility toward the person we are in conflict with. Good processing causes us to look at ourselves and see in the light of God's truth in a situation.

5. When someone comes to you with a problem with someone else, be a wise counselor and a peacemaker.
Remember the enemy is a divider. He is constantly trying to instigate anger and division. As disciples of Jesus, we want to see people resolve issues. Unresolved issues bring about bitterness that can poison the person we care about in the conflict. Hebrews 12:14–15 says:

> Make every effort to live in peace with everyone and to be holy; without holiness no one will see the Lord. See to it that no one falls short of the grace of God and that no bitter root grows up to cause trouble and defile many.

Gossip is spreading negative stuff about someone to other people without the intent to get help in resolving the problem. Slander is telling lies about someone meant to hurt them or their reputation. Both are toxic. As Christian leaders, make sure you encourage people to deal with the issue and do what is right, no matter what they think the other person will do. Offer to go with them, if appropriate, after they take the first right step. Remember, I am talking primarily about the church and family here, but much of this can also apply at any workplace as well. If you're dealing with a non-Christian person or work environment, resolution may be more difficult. At the least, you can pray for them and ask the Lord to heal hearts that might have already been poisoned. Remember that a lack of forgiveness is like drinking a poison yourself and hoping it will kill someone else.

6. There is a time to go your own ways.

As I have written before, we can do all we know how to do. We can pray, try to reconcile, and sometimes still end up having to go our separate ways. We see Paul and Barnabas do this (Acts 15:36–41). If these godly guys couldn't always seem to figure it out, then we should probably have the expectation that some work arrangements can't always be worked out. Sometimes people just don't have the same vision. Sometimes your conscience will not let you get away with what someone else's will. As a leader, there are people you may have to reposition or even fire, perhaps because:

- They are not designed to do what they need to do on your team.
- They don't have the passion for the job they need to do on your team.
- Your two personalities clash; you love them, but the chemistry makes it harder than it should be.
- Your communication styles don't work together.
- As I already mentioned, sometimes there is immaturity on one or both parts.

There are more reasons for sure, but sometimes things just aren't working. As believers we aspire to be different from the way the world works, and we need to be willing to die to ourselves when it's a problem of pride or misunderstanding. Going our own ways should be the last thing we do, but if we do, we need to leave the other in the Lord's hands as his servant and child. Remember to be careful with another person's child. If you must fire them, do it in a way you honor the parent (in this case our heavenly Father). Scripture tells us that, as much as it depends on us, we should live at peace with all people (Romans 12:18). This is true even when it comes time to separate and go our own ways.

There are also times when a person we thought was mature in the faith and worth adding to the team and engaging in relationship ends up fooling us. Or sometimes they weren't fooling us, but over time they changed. Paul anticipated this problem while giving his farewell address to the elders in Ephesus. They wept together and seemed to be on the same team. Yet Paul predicted that some from their very number would become wolves in sheep's clothing and draw people away (Acts 20:29–30). In this case, a shepherd must protect the sheep by taking on the wolf. Scripture gives us guidance when it concerns those we are in relationship with but have become a problem. Recall the steps from Matthew 18 we discussed above. Titus 3:10–11 gives specified advice when it comes to divisive people:

> Warn a divisive person once, and then warn them a second time. After that, have nothing to do with them. You may be sure that such people are warped and sinful; they are self-condemned.

Scripture reveals that Paul had to name problem people and warn the flock about them (e.g., 2 Timothy 4:14–15). John had to name a leader in the church who had become divisive (3 John 1:9–10). There is even a time to discipline an elder when his sin has been well-established by two or three witnesses, and then to bring it before the whole church as a warning to everyone (1 Timothy 5:19–25). I believe in relationships, but I do not believe in preserving the relationship at all costs. There are times we even need to disengage from those who are publicly claiming Christ but are involved in flagrant sins. 1 Corinthians 5:11 says that "you must not associate with anyone who claims to be a brother or sister but is sexually immoral or greedy, an idolater or slanderer, a drunkard or swindler. Do not even eat with such people." I can pray for them and love them from a distance, but I can't pretend they're right with God and go on legitimizing their charade. I can hope they come to their senses, but there are times when decisions need to be made and boundaries need to be set for the protection of yourself, your family, your children, and the church.

When it comes to backing out of relationships, here are some safeguards I'll offer as ways to make sure you are thinking biblically about this rather than emotionally:

1. Make sure your purpose is not to destroy the other but is really about the good of the family of God and about the person's reputation and restoration.
2. Follow the Matthew 18 principle. First, go to the person alone.
3. Get wise counsel from someone not emotionally tied to the situation to help you see if you are taking things wrong. If possible, it needs to be a mature person who can help bring reconciliation.
4. Bring a mature person with the heart of reconciliation into the equation—rather than just someone on your own side.
5. In the church, elders are supposed to ensure people are following the process and then be willing to be part of the process in its final stages.

6. Be open to reconciliation. Have a heart bent toward restoration.

7. Regardless of the outcome, continue to do the Lord's work. Don't allow the past to drive your life; go forward doing the Lord's will for your life.

I have had many battles in my life. In some ways, I am not the easiest person in the world to be in relationship with. I am a wrestler with a fighter mentality. In my life, I have had to work hard on my relationships, and I am so blessed to have many friends who have fought for relationship with me. I still have some relationships from my past that are still unresolved. I think and pray about these often. I know in heaven it will be figured out, but I sure would like to see restoration happen here first. When (not if) failure happens—whether on my, their, or our part—I often feel ashamed and want to give up. But then Jesus reminds me that I am broken. Everyone is. There is a devil who seeks to divide us. We also live in a relationship-killing culture.

I am reminded that I can aspire to something and fail. This does not mean I am a hypocrite. A hypocrite is an actor pretending they are something they are not. A person who fails is simply human. And thank the Lord we are covered by his grace. What do we do when we fail? One of my favorite verses says that "though the righteous fall seven times, they rise again" (Proverbs 24:16a). In other words, he falls down seven times but gets up eight. With the Lord's help, I can do that.

A PERSON WHO FAILS IS SIMPLY HUMAN.

A TRUST THAT CARRIES US THROUGH LIFE

Here is a principle our staff has heard a thousand times. Some people assume that friendship is based on being in relationship with someone we never argue with or experience conflict with. My view of real friendship is quite different. In my way of thinking, I don't actually know if you are my friend until we have been in a disagreement.

Some people might not be as broken as I am, so they have more friends they've never disagreed with. But for me, I know that if you really know me, you will see my weaknesses. I know we will disagree on something at some point if we are choosing to work or do life together. Why? Because we have different giftings, different personalities, different preferences, different paces, and so on. We also have a sinful nature. When a disagreement occurs and we both work to honestly reconcile, then we'll be able in the future to put aside our pretend faces and talk about real things. On that side of this type of relational threshold, I know you are courageous and will tell me when I am off base, and I will tell you the same.

All of this to say, when we have been through battles together and are still standing side-by-side, there will be a trust that carries us through life. That kind of relationship isn't easy, but it's worth it. Those are the kinds of relationships you want in your life. Helping us get through the rough patches takes relationships that have been through ups and downs together. It will take leaders who have learned to go first in relationships, work through the conflict, and come out the other side stronger together.

A PRINCIPLES FOR CONFLICT EXERCISE

Conflicts will be a part of any leadership team. It should be on our priority list to deal with, rather than something we run away from or act like doesn't exist. Here are guidelines I recommend for your team. Review them and ask if you want to add to them or take away from them. Create the list of principles for conflict that your team will adopt and follow.

1. Deal with issues as they come up honestly and quickly.
2. Deal with the issue privately before you bring someone else into the equation (exceptions may exist when dealing with someone of the opposite sex).
3. Work on not becoming defensive. Celebrate the courage it took to be honest.
4. After there is a confrontation, go back later to check on how the other is doing.
5. When someone comes to you with a problem with someone else, be a wise counselor and a peacemaker.
6. There is a time to go your own ways.

11

SOME QUESTIONS AND ANSWERS

Over the years I have received some great questions concerning the practicality of implementing Jesus' disciple making lifestyle in the church. Remember, I believe that every church leader should be making disciples themselves just as Jesus did. Yes, he spoke to crowds, but he did his greatest work in a small group and in one-on-one conversations. I think under normal circumstances this is the best way for us to disciple people as well.

> JESUS DID HIS GREATEST WORK IN A SMALL GROUP AND IN ONE-ON-ONE CONVERSATIONS.

As church leaders, we must have an organized system and process by which believers can experience large group, as well as small group, engagement. So in our church, we do a large group meeting we call our "weekend services," and we also have mid-sized group programming that deals with all kinds of ministry goals (e.g., women's ministry, men's ministry, recovery ministry, sports and outdoors, benevolence, etc.).

However, everything in our church leads to *relational discipleship groups*. In these groups, we make sure we have a leader who has been trained with our doctrine, language, and methods for leading. We have approved curriculum. We have support and accountability for the small group leaders. But again, everything funnels down to the relationships that happen in these life groups.

In this final chapter, I want to deal with some of these questions I get concerning small groups because most church leaders have not dealt with groups at the kind of relational disciple making level we use at Real Life. Our church hosts experiential trainings to show people how to lead a disciple making small group rather than just a social group or a study group that only passes on knowledge. When church leaders begin to get it and live it out, relational disciple making changes the whole culture of their churches. With this in mind, let me answer some of the questions I get asked most often by church leaders at our conferences.

I want to try to focus in on what I really mean versus what you might assume I mean. Sometimes when people haven't had the opportunity to see a leader live out what they are trying to teach in person, they build a lifestyle based on what they think it would look like and miss some of the subtleties. Or they create some impractical and infeasible way of doing something that leaves them disappointed in themselves or others. This is why discipleship in person is so important because it clears up the ambiguity. But I'll try to be as helpful as I can be in describing how it works. Let's walk through some of the best questions I get and then give some practical feasible answers.

Q. You said that discipleship is a relational process, but then you have fifteen people in your life group. How do you disciple fifteen people if it takes personal relational investment? Wouldn't that take up your entire work week?

When we think of Jesus' disciples, we often think of the Twelve that he chose in Luke 6:12–16. However, if you read carefully, you will discover that he had far more than twelve that were considered disciples. On one occasion, he sent out seventy-two of his disciples by twos (Luke 10). He had a secret disciple named Joseph (John 19:38). There were female disciples who went with him as he traveled. Mary, Martha, and Lazarus were considered disciples of Jesus.

All these and more were all called his disciples even though they spent less personal time with him than the Twelve did. Jesus was then able to go to the next level of discipleship with the Twelve. And as you go through the Gospels, you discover that he even went further into relationship and intentional training with three of the Twelve: Peter, James, and John. When three thousand people were baptized into Christ in a single day, they too were all disciples, but not all of them would have had direct interaction with the Twelve. As an example, Paul wrote to all the disciples in Ephesus but then specifically to its leader Timothy with whom he had spent the most time.

My point is that you can make disciples in your small group of fifteen even though the amount of time you spend with each of them won't all be the same. There will be a few you really go deeper with. Especially in groups with both men and women, we must be careful and appropriate when we spend time with the opposite sex. In my life group, I am discipling, to one degree or another, all of the people in it (men and women and even the kids who come). But since I'm a guy, my deepest connections in the group are going to be with other guys.

I am making disciples when I lead the group because I am intentionally leading toward an end goal. I am pointing them to Jesus and teaching them to abide in him through how I teach and what I teach them to do on their own. Yet not everyone will get the same amount of attention from me. Authors/church leaders Bobby Harrington and Alex Absalom created the following helpful diagram focusing on the different levels of Jesus' discipling relationships in their book *Discipleship That Fits: The Five Kinds of Relationships God Uses to Help Us Grow.*

JESUS AND THE CROWDS — PUBLIC

JESUS AND THE 70 — SOCIAL

JESUS AND THE 12 — PERSONAL

JESUS AND THE 3 — TRANSPARENT

JESUS AND THE FATHER — DIVINE

DISCIPLESHIP.ORG

I bear these levels in mind in my discipling relationships. I have a handful of people I would consider in my "transparent" space. My life group fits the "personal" space. I also serve alongside others in the more "social" space. But I can only have so many deep relationships. When it comes to my life group of twelve to fifteen, I have differing levels of relationships. But the goal is to develop each of them into disciple makers and cultivate relationships between those in the group, facilitating relationships between the more mature and the less mature. As I encourage the older, or more mature, to invest in the younger, they both grow from the interaction. I also choose to spend more time with a few of them personally because I see them as leaders of the next group. When a problem arises for someone in the group, I might appoint one of the other future leaders to help them and then debrief how it went.

It is worth noting there may be seasons in your life when you can't disciple as many people as you might at other times. Maybe you're parenting very young children who need more of your time and focus, or maybe you are an adult who has taken on the role of caretaker for an aging parent. Regardless of the season of life you are in, you are still a disciple and a disciple maker. It doesn't matter if you're pouring into one or two people or fifteen.

> **IT DOESN'T MATTER IF YOU'RE POURING INTO ONE OR TWO PEOPLE OR FIFTEEN.**

Q. *How do you intentionally make disciples and send them out to make disciples and still have real friendships? Do you just make a whole new group of best friends?*

Jesus told his Twelve that they had become his friends rather than just servants (John 15:14). Jesus combined his discipleship with genuine friendship. For those who say a leader must choose leadership or friendship but cannot have both with the same people, I very much disagree.

It's not always easy, but friendship with those who disciple can and should be done. Some of my best friends became disciple makers in a group I led. Now they have gone on to lead other groups and even churches across the country, so that can leave a void. But they are still my closest friends. Over the years, we developed more than just a disciple/disciple maker relationship. We had a lot in common and went through a lot together that led to a deeper connection. Yes, they moved from my group, but not from my life. We hunt together, talk weekly, and spend family time as friends. Two close friends still in the area used to be in my life group, but now they are leading their own groups. But we still meet early on Wednesdays to discuss how our groups and lives are going.

So, yes, you may multiply a group, but you don't have to lose the relationship.

Q. When you start a new group, do you only ask people you like or know into the group? If not, how do you become friends with new people all the time?

When I start a new group, I keep some of the families from my old group with us and I invite others. Sometimes it's people I know and sometimes it's not. One constant is that I try to keep some of my wife's closest friends who offer spiritual support for her because while I get to go to work and be with some of my closest friends there, she doesn't have that opportunity, and this group is her spiritual family.

I don't ever intend to unseat my close friends from their role in my life with these new folks. I am still doing life with my closest friends in a variety of ways that extend past our life group. Remember, many Christians do not have real Christian friends because they only attend church and haven't let church flow into their lives. Their lives are too busy to have spent the intentional time it takes to have made the friends they could be making there. So I make sure the people in the group know that I am inviting them into discipleship as well as friendship in general, but with no promises of becoming best friends at the same time. I do my best to set the right expectations in the group and tell them I too am very busy trying to have a balanced life.

In essence I am inviting them into a discipleship relationship with me and a spiritual family relationship with one another. During our time together, I work hard at connecting people in my group to one another. Some may develop into lifelong friends, and I can be a spiritual parent that helps to connect their need to people who are learning to meet it and vice versa. By creating a safe place for people to learn what that looks like and then begin to experience it, many of them do become lifelong friends with one another.

Q. Is there a way to lead your life group that makes it easier for people to connect relationally outside of the group?

If the discipleship group is led well, people will learn to dive into the Scriptures as well as tell their stories and share their concerns and pray. Yet it's important to remember that though the small group is much more relational than a weekend service, it still cannot be the end-all-be-all of relational discipleship.

A good small group does several things within the group that lead beyond the group time:

A. The small group gives me the ability to learn more about where people are in their spiritual development as they answer questions and share honestly with others. It helps me to know what steps to take next—maybe a phone call or a meeting for coffee later.

B. The small group allows people to get to know each other so that when I discern an issue someone in the group has, I can ask a more mature believer to connect after the group with them. Remember, you are facilitating the next step for those in your group, and part of that is helping people connect to one another.

C. Remember that when you allow someone else to play a part in other people's lives, this gives them the ability to grow in their skills and relate to others for everyone's benefit. Our job is to create disciples who can create disciples. A quick phone call after these kinds of interactions to debrief how it went helps the apprentice (future leader) grow in their relating and coaching skills. This creates a relational environment and support in the group rather than putting too much weight on you.

D. As people share in the group, they will start to find they have common interests and issues with those in the group. This leads to further conversations outside the group.

E. As I deal with things in the group relationally, this gives the apprentices the opportunity to see how to deal with things so we can debrief it later.

F. We spend time doing fun things together with our whole families so that relational ties are built. These times give me an opportunity to see how people interact in real time with others in their families. Now I can know what to deal with in real life because I have seen how they really are instead of just the impression they want to make.

Q. How can church leaders live a balanced life between ministry and authentic relationships?

So often, pastors struggle to live a lifestyle that allows them to thrive as people. Over the years, our team has put together a framework for living a balanced lifestyle. We want to create an environment in our church that allows people to have a sustainable lifestyle while honoring God and the responsibilities he's given us in both the church and the home. We also understand the health issues that can result from being spiritually and relationally unhealthy. With this in mind, we help people create both a Ministry Plan and a Personal Ministry Plan.

THE MINISTRY PLAN

During a church leader's forty-hour work week, we think in terms of the ministry we lead. (You'll see below why I highly recommend keeping it at forty hours.) During the work week, we plan messages and lead volunteers and paid staff if we have them. We think in terms of training leaders, creating goals, and reaching them as a team. We train people and look at the finances with stewardship in mind. We do pastoral duties like weddings, funerals, calling on the sick, and so on. My point is that just as people in our church have a work life, we have one as well. So it's important for each church leader to think through their ministry well and map out a plan that helps them work hard and effectively but also keep within boundaries that allow them to thrive in their "personal ministry" outside of their work.

At our church, we expect our people to have a personal ministry as well, which includes attending church services, serving, and being in deep relationship from which discipleship flows. We need to remember that others have a work life too, and yet we are also asking them to serve in the church and make disciples in relationship. This has a time piece to it that impacts their lives. It's healthy for church leaders to recognize what we're calling others to and to intentionally carve out both a Ministry Plan and a Personal Ministry Plan, ensuring that neither is getting short-changed.

THE PERSONAL MINISTRY PLAN

When a person works for a living full time, it takes at least forty hours a week—very often more. Likewise, the spiritual family as God designed it takes committed time as well as proximity. On average, we at Real Life ask people to spend upwards of ten hours a week as a part of the church family. Sometimes there will be more and sometimes less, but commitment to spiritual relationships is important. Here's a typical breakdown of a Personal Ministry Plan for one of our leaders:

- Quiet time with the Lord, journaling, etc. – approximately two hours per week
- Church services on the weekend – two hours (including time to serve and/or talk with people)
- Small group – two hours (If you are leading, this gives added time to prepare.)
- One-on-one conversations, including texting, phone calls, etc., to check on your brothers and sisters if they are missing or struggling – one hour a week
- Sometimes there is a spiritual emergency for someone in your life group, and it may take more intentional time.
- You want to be available for relational time as needed, spending time with your Christian friends in a variety of different ways that don't feel like work at all: games, coffee, camping, and so on.

Again, we call this the Personal Ministry Plan and encourage everyone in the church to design one. For those who are called into full-time ministry, we ask them to continue with their Personal Ministry Plan but now replace their work plan with their Ministry Plan.

We want our people to have healthy, balanced lives that allow them to run the marathon, not just a spiritual sprint to exhaustion. By making sure that every staff member is living out their Personal Ministry Plan as well as their Ministry Plan, we see to it that relational discipleship is being lived out in every part of our team. Our leaders are not asking others to do what they themselves are not doing.

I'll end with a question I'm not typically asked, but I know a lot of people have it in the back of their minds. So here goes:

Q. When do I graduate from having to personally make disciples?

Often, church leaders assume they have graduated from making disciples personally because now they lead a disciple making organization (the church). When this assumption takes root, several issues arise.

- You lose the people who could best show others how to best do what you are asking others to do.
- You lose your credibility because you are not doing what you ask others to do. (Remember, they have jobs too.)
- Your leaders lose what made them effective leaders in the first place. Relational discipleship is what grew them and sustained them as people.
- They begin to live on stories of what they used to see rather than what they see currently in the lives of others. I have heard so many pastors talk about old stories of when they used to do ministry at the front lines and now all they do is work in an office and don't get to see God work any longer. People need to see life change. It fuels us and reminds us of why we do what we do.

- They lose touch with the real issues their people are dealing with, and this affects how they do ministry. So many pastors preach sermons about what they think their people are dealing with rather than what they really are. They also don't know how their sermons are affecting people because they don't get to hear how people are hearing them and are practically using the messages. They no longer do ministry in a way that their family engages with (they leave it at work), so they're not modeling discipleship or creating discipling opportunities for their spouse and kids.

To this day, I have a forty-hour work week that I monitor closely. If I work too many hours one week, I have to make it up the next by cutting back. I've got to keep it at forty hours because, in the same week, I lead a life group with my wife. I have a Wednesday morning men's group with some of the men in my life group, as well as other men that I invite to go deeper into specific accountability areas. I have a Thursday afternoon group where I invite future leaders. Many in that group are now in full-time ministry or church planters, etc.

By monitoring my time effectively, I have time to spend with my wife and kids and grandkids as well. It may seem difficult to balance ministry, disciple making, and the rest of life. But as a church leader, if I am discipling others well, I have more people to share the ministry load with. As they grow, I am not needed in many places I once had to stand in. As people do ministry together, the work is more effective, and people pour into one another as they go on the mission together. It doesn't feel like work alone when we do it together as friends.

LIVING AND LEADING FROM RELATIONSHIP

Let's get to the point. If you're a church leader, I'm asking you to live and lead from relationship. There are too many lonely church leaders and too few mature disciples being made; neither group will be able to provide what each other needs until church leaders begin living and leading from relationship. Here are the five shifts that will allow you to live and lead from relationship:

RelationShift 1: From Feed Me to Fellowship
RelationShift 2: From Friendliness to Love
RelationShift 3: From Recognition to Realness
RelationShift 4: From Skeptical to Safe
RelationShift 5: From Idea to Implementation

Yet I know what a lot of you are thinking:

I understand this, but it won't work in my situation.

You might think, *my people will not go for this.* Many pastors must answer to a congregational vote to get and keep their job. They have a group of people who are trained to expect certain things and if the pastor doesn't deliver, they'll lose their job. That is a real thing, believe it or not. But remember, your calling to the ministry wasn't a call to make people happy but to make the Lord happy. Saying no to your people is not the same thing as saying no to God.

You might think, *No one has shown me how to do this, and I don't want to look like a fool.* I would respond that faith and obedience are risky. But I would add that old dogs can learn new tricks—I have seen it a thousand times. Remember that your people who decide to become disciples of Jesus are risking too. They are trying to do something they have not done before, and the potential for failure is there for them too. You might say the wrong thing at times or miss something along the way. You will make mistakes and learn as you go. Remember, you cannot get good at any sport merely by sitting on the bench. You have to be allowed in the game and then get

YOU CANNOT GET GOOD AT ANY SPORT MERELY BY SITTING ON THE BENCH.

coached. Walking with integrity means you are willing to do what you are asking others to do. If you are a leader, you go first. That is what it means to be a leader.

You might think, *My elders* [or whatever you call the leaders you answer to] *will not allow me to make changes to the whole church.* I would suggest that you do your best to live up to expectations they have, while still going first in personally living out these differences we've talked about in front of them. If you become relationally trustworthy, you may be surprised what ends up changing. Often, not always, if you do the right thing, you might end up getting the right thing back. If you're afraid that you may have to do your personal relational disciple making on your own time, recall that this is exactly what you're asking the other people in your church to do as well.

You might think, *But I have been hurt by sharing what is real about me to others.* Of course you have. But loneliness can hurt worse. And the blessings that come with realness are so much richer than the shallow praise that comes from name recognition. Some will respond and real friendships will be forged.

The most important answer to all our misgivings is that we live and lead from relationship because that's what Jesus did for us. It won't be easy, and you will get hurt at times, but start with your family and with those who are willing to go with you. When we quit trying, we miss out on those future relationships Jesus has in store for us later down the road. We also miss out on helping others discover what they were missing because we did not persevere. And if you try and no one is willing to be relationally discipled by you, then it could mean you have to ask yourself some tough questions about your leadership. Here's the sequence: we need to go first in the journey toward maturity ourselves, then help the body of Christ become mature as the Lord allows.

What I'm describing in this book works. It's nothing new; it's what Jesus modeled for us. Yet I should mention that some people will grow dissatisfied with a church that centers on relational disciple making because they are not getting what they had expected or hoped for. I can't tell you how many times someone has told me I needed to preach on a certain topic because of a particular situation or fascination that was happening in their lives. They believe that if the sermons don't hit on their specific felt needs, the church isn't feeding them, so they insist upon going somewhere they can be spoon fed what they feel they need. Then, after looking around at other churches for a while, many conclude that no one is being truly fed in them either, and they eventually leave the church altogether. So many Christians today fit into this category of de-churched.

To people who come at me with this attitude, I explain that they are not the only ones in the church and that others are dealing with different issues. I also explain that everything does not need to fit into one spiritual dinner once a week. Everyone is at different stages of spiritual

EVERYTHING DOES NOT NEED TO FIT INTO ONE SPIRITUAL DINNER ONCE A WEEK.

growth and dealing with different things. So, along with the "all-church dinner" that happens weekly in the weekend service, they have a responsibility to learn to feed themselves to grow. Just as we eat several times a day physically, we need to feed ourselves spiritually in more than one way. I tell them they can do studies on particular issues, reading great books on the specific subjects that affect them. Their daily Bible reading and devotion time are important for spiritual feeding too. Listening to Christian music and hearing preaching on the radio can all be a part of it too. They can download sermons from other pastors and listen to podcasts daily.

But very importantly, they will remain malnourished until they learn to take responsibility for being in relationship contexts where those who are more mature can help feed them—and where they can grow into disciple makers themselves.

As we at Real Life work hard to live out these principles, we see not only a new way of life emerging that strengthens our church and other churches, but we also see people on the outside coming to faith. Living and leading from relationship is worth it, and you'll need to remind yourself of this often. When things get really busy, it's easy for us as pastors to get pulled back into our old mechanical boxes of doing things. The people in many of our congregations have been trained to want certain things, and it takes a long time and a lot of support to get us out of just giving them what they feel they need.

So I am praying that you take some time to intentionally pursue this way of doing life and church leadership. If you decide to follow Jesus in this area, you will begin to experience life and ministry more richly, even as it means more investment of time and energy. The people you lead will begin taking you more seriously because you are going through life with integrity. But even more importantly, people will see Jesus more clearly because you're doing more than talking about him; you're showing Jesus to them through the clearest and fullest communication possible: relationships.

I pray that you will take steps to live your life the way God intended and lead the way for others to follow.

FINAL RELATIONSHIFT TEAM EXERCISE

It is easy to read a book and find many valuable principles. But we often just obtain the information without changing anything or adopting the practices that we have read about and want to follow. As a team, review the five exercises that accompany each of the five shifts (page 49, 77, 117, 156, and 188).

Now pick three practices or guidelines from these exercises that you will adopt immediately. List them below.

APPENDIX A

Fifty-Nine "One Another's" in the New Testament

1. "Be at peace with each other" (Mark 9:50b).
2. "Wash one another's feet" (John 13:14b).
3. ". . . Love one another . . ." (John 13:34).
4. "Love one another" (John 13:34b).
5. "Love one another" (John 13:35b).
6. "Love each other . . ." (John 15:12b).
7. "Love each other" (John 15:17).
8. "Be devoted to one another in love" (Romans 12:10a).
9. "Honor one another above yourselves (Romans 12:10b).
10. "Live in harmony with one another" (Romans 12:16a).
11. ". . . Love one another . . ." (Romans 13:8).
12. "Stop passing judgment on one another" (Romans 14:13a).
13. "Accept one another, then, just as Christ accepted you" (Romans 15:7a).
14. "Instruct one another" (Romans 15:14b).
15. "Greet one another with a holy kiss" (Romans 16:16a).
16. "When you gather to eat, you should all eat together" (1 Corinthians 11:33b).
17. "Have equal concern for each other" (1 Corinthians 12:25b).

18. "Greet one another with a holy kiss"
    (1 Corinthians 16:20b).
19. "Greet one another with a holy kiss"
    (2 Corinthians 13:12).
20. "Serve one another humbly in love" (Galatians 5:13b).
21. "If you bite and devour each other. . . you will be
    destroyed by each other" (Galatians 5:15).
22. "Let us not become conceited, provoking and envying
    each other" (Galatians 5:26).
23. "Carry each other's burdens" (Galatians 6:2a).
24. "Be patient, bearing with one another in love"
    (Ephesians 4:2b).
25. "Be kind and compassionate to one another"
    (Ephesians 4:32a).
26. ". . . Forgiving each other . . ." (Ephesians 4:32).
27. "Speak to one another with psalms, hymns, and songs
    from the Spirit" (Ephesians 5:19a).
28. "Submit to one another out of reverence for Christ"
    (Ephesians 5:21).
29. "In humility value others above yourselves"
    (Philippians 2:3b).
30. "Do not lie to each other" (Colossians 3:9a).
31. "Bear with each other" (Colossians 3:13a).
32. ". . . Forgive one another if any of you has a grievance
    against some . . ." (Colossians 3:13).
33. "Let the message of Christ dwell among you richly as you
    teach . . . one another" (Colossians 3:16a).
34. "Admonish one another" (Colossians 3:16b).
35. "May the Lord make your love increase and overflow for
    each other" (1 Thessalonians 3:12a).
36. "Love each other" (1 Thessalonians 4:9b).

37. "Encourage one another" (1 Thessalonians 4:18a).

38. "Encourage one another" (1 Thessalonians 5:11a).

39. "Build each other up . . ." (1 Thessalonians 5:11b).

40. "Encourage one another daily" (Hebrews 3:13a).

41. "Spur one another on toward love and good deeds" (Hebrews 10:24b).

42. ". . . Encouraging one another . . ." (Hebrews 10:25).

43. "Do not slander one another" (James 4:11a).

44. "Don't grumble against one another" (James 5:9a).

45. "Confess your sins to each other" (James 5:16a).

46. "Pray for each other . . ." (James 5:16b).

47. "Love one another deeply, from the heart" (1 Peter 1:22b).

48. "Love one another, be compassionate and humble" (1 Peter 3:8b).

49. "Love each other deeply" (1 Peter 4:8a).

50. "Offer hospitality to one another without grumbling" (1 Peter 4:9).

51. "Each of you should use whatever gift you have received to serve others" (1 Peter 4:10a).

52. ". . . Clothe yourselves with humility toward one another . . ." (1 Peter 5:5).

53. "Greet one another with a kiss of love" (1 Peter 5:14a).

54. "Love one another" (1 John 3:11b).

55. "Love one another" (1 John 3:23b).

56. "Love one another" (1 John 4:7a).

57. "Love one another" (1 John 4:11b).

58. "Love one another" (1 John 4:12b).

59. "Love one another" (2 John 5b).

APPENDIX B
American Idol Exercise

Do you remember the old version of the *American Idol* singing competition where they showcased people who thought they could sing but really couldn't? I thought it was all a joke until sadly I watched many of these people being undone by rejection. They had actually thought they could sing, either because they were tone deaf and couldn't hear themselves, or because the ones who had told them they could sing were also tone deaf. Or, in other cases, the people who told them they were good loved them so much they just couldn't be honest. Or maybe they only saw the heart of the person and it changed how their ears heard things. Love covers a multitude of sins (1 Peter 4:8), even musical ones.

In the same way, it is possible that you have people who love you so much and understand your heart so well that they don't take your shortcomings as seriously as those who don't know your heart. If your team grows, there will be people who come in who never get the chance to know your heart and will judge it by your imperfect actions.

It's also possible that those around you won't tell you your flaws and shortcomings because it's not safe to share without ramifications. So you go into the world without knowing you are deficient in one or more important areas of your life. If your weakness is in the relational category, it will hinder not only your work life but also your more important relational life as well. You may not know that you are creating an untrustworthy and non-relational environment around yourself. Part of discipleship is to help people come to know the truth about themselves so that they can grow in relational success for themselves and those around them. This will mean that we need trustworthy leaders, trustworthy followers, and trustworthy peers and friends to help us.

Often, we build teams around us that have the same holes we have. Birds of a feather can flock together. So it's important that you determine the areas accurately that create wholeness. Sometimes this means you need to add someone to your round of counsel that you don't currently have. I found this to be true when our young church started around twenty-five years ago. One of my friends and a pastor Aaron Couch and I were both young and could see only what we could see with young idealistic eyes. Someone suggested that we seek some counsel from an older, more mature Christian to help us understand how older believers were perceiving us. It was so helpful that we decided to bring that older counsel onto the team. It made us better.

People will become willing to help us if we become trustworthy and safe to help. Closing the gap in your self-awareness may initially be painful, but the long-term good for you and those in your life is immeasurable. This is a part of the journey that is not only biblical but very rewarding when you work through it.

With this in mind, let's take a look at the bullseye graph again.

BOSS/LEADER

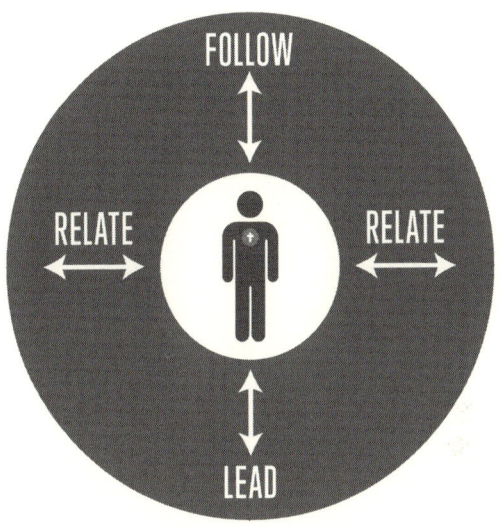

In the spaces below you will see the "Big 7" trustworthiness attributes I talked about in Chapter 7. Rank yourself between one and ten for each of the seven. A ten represents a high level of trust your boss would have for you and a one represents a low level of trust. Then, in the second column, ask yourself what your boss would answer for the same area. Notice that I did not ask you to answer for your boss. There is usually a gap between what you would say about yourself and how others perceive you. Remember, a mature disciple of Jesus doesn't respond to conflict by complaining about the other person; they first go to reconcile it to the best of their ability. They seek to become trustworthy and safe themselves.

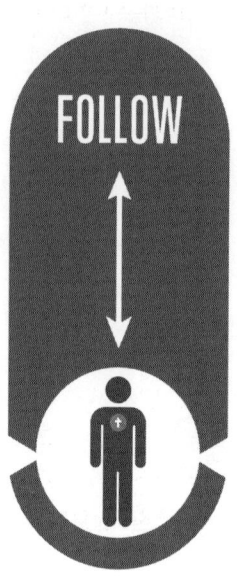

FOLLOW

1. *You are courageous.* Your view of you: _____. Your boss's view of you: _____.

2. *You are honest.* Your view of you: _____. Your boss's view of you: _____.

3. *You are humble.* Your view of you: _____. Your boss's view of you: _____.

4. *You are loyal.* Your view of you: _____. Your boss's view of you: _____.

5. *You give wise counsel.* Your view of you: _____. Your boss's view of you: _____.

6. *You are a reconciler.* Your view of you: _____. Your boss's view of you: _____.

7. *You are a forgiver.* Your view of you: _____. Your boss's view of you: _____.

I have seen many who thought their leaders would trust them, but they don't. Often, the reason the boss doesn't tell you is because they don't like conflict. It may mean they have tried to share their issues with you but, in their view, you didn't listen. For whatever reason, they have put you in a box and deal with you accordingly. Now, they mainly just put up with you, or they won't let you lead in certain situations because they don't trust you. And the sad thing is you have no idea.

In other cases, you may be incredibly hard on yourself, and you just assume those around you don't trust or approve of you. In my dad's later years, he moved here to northern Idaho where I am the senior pastor to be a part of our staff team. He has done several jobs here and has been a blessing in so many ways. Now, my dad grew up in a strict disciplinarian's home. He never heard his dad say he was proud of him or that he loved him—ever. If he got out of line, he was either strongly disciplined or ignored. My grandfather didn't say much (he had his own family history to deal with too), and wherever there is a gap in communication the devil loves to fill in the blanks by helping us assume things. So for my dad's entire life, that voice in his head has spoken disapproval to him. The default voice in his head is one of disapproval unless you tell him he is doing a good job.

I, on the other hand, was told at least once every day of my life that I was loved by my dad. I heard, "I am proud of you" so many times I could never put a number on it. The voice in my head is saying something completely different. In fact I tend to think I am doing a good job unless you tell me otherwise. So now, let's put us together in a work environment.

Here is the scene: I was running around with my hair on fire trying to put out fires everywhere because of the rapid growth of our church. I brought my dad on to take care of some of the fires so I could try to concentrate on the others. I was so sure he was doing a good job that I wouldn't even go over to where he was fighting fires because I knew he had it handled. I was thinking, *I am so glad he is over there! He is doing such a good job!*

I was *thinking* it.

One day, I was blown away when my father made an appointment with me and came into my office with what looked like a real problem. He said, "Jim, I came to ask you what I can do better so that I am not disappointing you." At first I thought he was joking. Then he began to share what he thought I thought of him based on his performance. I was completely dumbfounded. I discovered that the voice in my head toward him was completely different than the voice in his head toward himself.

Some of you have a voice in your head like my dad heard for decades. When you take this simple assessment, you put numbers that are far too low. The sad part about my dad is that he was doing a great job, but he didn't *feel* like he was trusted and loved. As leaders, we have to understand that what we think or feel is going on, in many cases, is not the truth. It's only in honest relationships that we discover what's really going on under the surface. This experience with my dad reinforced that I cannot trust my own understanding of things. I am so glad that my father made that appointment with me and asked me how I was seeing him and told me how he was seeing me. Then we got the chance to get rid of the communication gap so that our inner voices and the devil's deception couldn't fill the gap with lies.

Here is the point. In your relationship with your leader, making a point to create a safe place where coaching is desired and accepted can help you not only get the feedback you need but also the deeper relationships you were made for. When your boss sees you as humble and responsive, it opens the door to trustworthiness in a variety of ways.

PEERS/CO-WORKERS

Now, let's repeat the process while assessing your side-to-side relationships. You may not think this level of intentionality matters in your relationships with peers, but remember that wherever we work, live, or play, we are on a mission with Jesus for the salvation of people. How we are perceived by others affects not only our satisfaction in life but also our witness for Jesus.

1. *You are courageous.* Your view of you: _____. Their view of you: _____.
2. *You are honest.* Your view of you: _____. Their view of you: _____.
3. *You are humble.* Your view of you: _____. Their view of you: _____.

4. *You are loyal.* Your view of you: _____. Their view of you: _____.

5. *You give wise counsel.* Your view of you: _____. Their view of you: _____.

6. *You are a reconciler.* Your view of you: _____. Their view of you: _____.

7. *You are a forgiver.* Your view of you: _____. Their view of you: _____.

THOSE YOU LEAD

Now, let's do the same with those you lead. Do your people follow you because you offer a paycheck? Do they follow you because they have to? Because you are the father or the husband? As disciples of Jesus, we are becoming more and more like Jesus. Because of the way Jesus led, people wanted to be with him. As we become more Christlike in our leadership, we are entrusted with more and gain greater influence for God's glory and the good of others, and even for our own good.

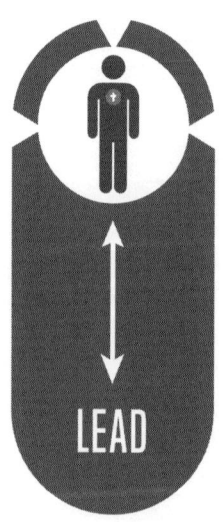

1. *You are courageous.* Your view of you: _____. Their view of you: _____.
2. *You are honest.* Your view of you: _____. Their view of you: _____.
3. *You are humble.* Your view of you: _____. Their view of you: _____.
4. *You are loyal.* Your view of you: _____. Their view of you: _____.
5. *You give wise counsel.* Your view of you: _____. Their view of you: _____.
6. *You are a reconciler.* Your view of you: _____. Their view of you: _____.
7. *You are a forgiver.* Your view of you: _____. Their view of you: _____.

APPENDIX C

Expectations and Assumptions for Small Groups

EXPECTATIONS

At Real Life, we talk about what is expected in our small groups if they are to be safe and productive. We talk about how over-talking by one person can shut down openness for others. We talk about not trying to fix someone in the group when they share what is going on. There is a time to help people see the truth of Scripture, but first we listen well and empathize (and that does not mean just agree with them). We talk about using "I" statements, being personal and transparent, rather than speaking in generalities. Here is the list of seven expectations we have for our small groups:[11]

1. Safe place – It needs to be an environment of realness, openness, and honesty.
2. No cross talk – Be considerate of others as they are sharing. No side conversations, checking phones, etc. while others are talking.
3. Listen. – Value one another by listening to what they're sharing.
4. No rescuing or fixing – We are not here to fix each other; Jesus does that part. Avoid the tendency to rescue when

someone is struggling to get the words out or is sharing a
struggle or conviction.

5. Use "I" statements. – It's easy to talk about the issues of
   others or respond with "we," "us," or "the church." For us
   to grow as disciples and build relationships, we need to use
   "I" statements.

6. Don't overtalk. – Be careful not to always be the first
   responder or regularly give long responses.

7. Fight for relationship. – When—not if—conflict or hurt
   feelings happen in the group, we commit to working hard
   to keep good relationships with each other.

ASSUMPTIONS

Here are some assumptions I lead groups with (and teach
other groups to follow as well) to help lead thoughtfully
and effectively:

1. Many of the new people probably have not been discipled
   to understand that God is just as serious about how we
   relate to one another as he is about the doctrine that we
   hold to.

2. Most believers were not discipled at home or in a church
   where relationship as God defines it was modeled. Most
   have gone to church but have never really *been* the
   church before.

3. Most Christians were not taught what real relationships
   look like in practical terms. They were not taught the rules
   of safe, godly relationships.

4. Even if they have been in my group before, or in another
   like it, people can still forget and flat out fail. We can
   forget the big dual purposes for our meeting: our ultimate

goal is to make friends and intentionally grow as mature disciples who can make disciples at the same time. We will need to be reminded because we can fall into our comfort zone and easily become reactionary and inconsistent.

5. Because people easily fall into unrealistic expectations, we talk through what we can expect from others in the group. We tell them we will make mistakes here (we will misunderstand, forget to follow through, say the wrong thing), and we will have to resolve conflict in a godly way.

6. Most of them have not been held accountable when they fell short and were not dealt with in a loving way that resulted in reconciliation.

7. Some will try to make the life group their only church experience, so I will reinforce again and again that being in church on the weekend is expected. And I will share that we all have gifts that can be used in various ways by the larger church. Some can serve in children's ministry or as a youth volunteer at times, etc.

In addition, I talk about my "Big 7" (see Chapter 7), so they know what I believe biblical trustworthiness includes. I vision cast that if we live out this kind of trustworthiness, then our group may be the safest place they have ever been. However, I make sure everyone has the right expectations. Though we aspire to this, we will sometimes fail. I then lay out how we will fight for relationships when, not if, we fail.

FIGHTING FOR RELATIONSHIPS

Few have been taught how to deal with conflict in a loving way. Christians can be cowards who cloak their cowardice in biblical-sounding language. Here are some of the statements I have heard over the years that not only frustrate me but make me sad:

- "The Bible says to forgive, so I just didn't deal with the issue and prayed about it instead." (Except they didn't forgive and now have the other person in a box they don't know they're in and can't get out of.)
- "The Lord is leading me to another church." (Except the Lord isn't leading them somewhere else if the reason they're leaving is anger they haven't tried to resolve. His Word tells us he wants us to reconcile rather than just take our ball and go home—or to another field to play.)
- "I was just telling them the truth! I didn't like what they did. They were wrong!" (Except we are called to be slow to speak and slow to become angry, and man's anger does not bring about the righteousness that God desires [James 1:19–20]. Showing judgment rather than a curious desire to understand does not bring reconciliation. We are to tell the truth in love.)

Because people so easily get scared when it comes to conflict, I especially hit on the inevitability of conflict that comes when people get together. Conflict will come. It's what we do with the conflict that can change our lives for the better.

We have different personalities, gifting abilities, perspectives, learning styles, conflict styles, and ways of defining words and using them. Added to this, we each have a self-centered, sinful nature that will threaten relationships in covert ways. Yes, if we are disciples of Jesus, we also have the Holy Spirit of God working within us to help us die to that self-absorbed part of us. But we still fail often. And if all that wasn't enough, as we have already discussed, we have a spiritual enemy who is at work to destroy relationships any way he can.

So I really try hard to help people understand what I wrote about in Chapter 7. We want people to become trustworthy and to learn to go first when there is conflict.

NOTES

FOREWORD

1. "ChurchPulse Weekly Conversations: Juli Wilson & Kayla Stoecklein on the Mental Health Struggles of Ministry," *Barna Research*, May 12, 2021, barna.com/research/cpw-wilson-stoecklein (accessed August 7, 2022).

2. "What Are 70% of Pastors Facing Right Now?" *Q Talk*, qideas.org/qtalks/what-are-70-of-pastors-facing-right-now (accessed August 7, 2022).

CHAPTER 3

3. Kelvin Teamer, *Kingdom Life: Experiencing God's Reign Through Love and Holiness* (Renew.org, 2021), 67.

CHAPTER 5

4. My son Christian and I each did a video series on this time of our lives. It is available with study guides from Right Now Media. We talked about our experiences during his struggle through addiction and rebellion—one from the perspective of a parent with a prodigal child and one with the perspective of the prodigal. See Christian Putman, "The Prodigal," rightnowmedia.org/Content/Series/439981, and Jim Putman, "Runaway," rightnowmedia.org/Content/Series/439982.

CHAPTER 6

5. Access our *Irreplaceable* docuseries and discussion guides at "The Irreplaceable Series: Opening the Discussion about Suicide," *Real Life Ministries*, https://realliferesources.org/pdf-resource/the-irreplaceable-series/ (accessed September 2, 2022).

6. "Suicide Statistics," American Foundation for Suicide Prevention, afsp.org/suicide-statistics/ (accessed September 2, 2022).

7. "Pastors Share Top Reasons They've Considered Quitting Ministry in the Past Year," *Barna Research*, April 27, 2022, barna.com/research/pastors-quitting-ministry/ (accessed September 2, 2022).

8. "The Magic Thread," in William J. Bennett, *The Book of Virtues: A Treasury of Great Moral Stories* (New York: Simon & Schuster, 1993), 57–63.

CHAPTER 7

9. For a downloadable PDF of my "Big 7," visit bit.ly/theBIG7.

CHAPTER 10

10. *Rocky III*, directed by Sylvester Stallone (Chartoff-Winkler Productions, 1982).

APPENDIX C: EXPECTATIONS AND ASSUMPTIONS FOR SMALL GROUPS

11. For a complete list, see "7 Guidelines for Small Group Discussions—Creating Safe Environments Where Relationships Can Grow," *Real Life Ministries*, realliferesources.

org/pdf-resource/12-guidelines-for-small-group-discussions/ (accessed September 9, 2022).

ABOUT THE AUTHOR

Jim Putman is the founder and senior pastor of Real Life Ministries in Post Falls, Idaho. Real Life Ministries began as a small group in 1998 and has grown to a membership of more than eight thousand people. The church was launched with a commitment to discipleship and the model of discipleship Jesus practiced, which is called "Relational Discipleship." Ninety percent of the people are active in small groups. *Outreach Magazine* continually lists Real Life Ministries among the top one hundred most influential churches in America.

Jim holds degrees from Boise State University and Boise Bible College. Each year his teaching ministry reaches hundreds of thousands across the nation through speaking at conferences, the web, radio, and weekend services. He is the author/co-author of six books: *Church Is a Team Sport, Real Life Discipleship, The Real Life Discipleship Workbook* (with Avery Willis and others), *The Power of Together Workbook, DiscipleShift* (with Bobby Harrington and Robert Coleman), *Hope for the Prodigal* (with Bill Putman), *The Revolutionary Disciple* (with Chad Harrington), and most recently, *The Disciple's Journey.* Jim's passion is discipleship through small groups. With his background in sports and coaching, he believes in the value of strong coaching as a means to disciple others. He lives with his wife and three sons in scenic northern Idaho.

biblically responsible investing

because we value our investors

Start investing today at **www.TheSolomonFoundation.org**

Made in the USA
Middletown, DE
28 March 2023

27312054R00142